THE WISDOM OF
LEADERSHIP

Gamla Stan 30/10-2013

THE WISDOM OF LEADERSHIP

TIMELESS PRINCIPLES FOR GREATER PURPOSE, PROSPERITY, AND PEACE OF MIND

Till Percy,

Du är en sann förebild för ett professionellt och gott ledarskap!

Författaren Per Winblad

Per Winblad

LIGHTHOUSE
HILL
PRESS

Beverly Hills, California

 Lighthouse Hill Press
269 S. Beverly Dr. #1065
Beverly Hills, CA 90212
Tel: (866) 234-0626
Fax: (310) 564-1991

Publisher's Cataloguing-in-Publication information

Winblad, Per.

The wisdom of leadership : timeless principles for greater purpose, prosperity & peace of mind / Per Winblad. -- 1st ed. -- Beverly Hills, CA : Lighthouse Hill Press, 2009.

p. ; cm.

ISBN: 978-0-9824732-5-2

1. Leadership. 2. Motivation (Psychology)
I. Title. II. Timeless principles for greater purpose, prosperity & peace of mind.

HD57.7 .W56 2009   2009927759
658.4092--dc22   0908

Book Consultant: Ellen Reid
Jacket Design: Chris Korblein
Interior Design and Layout: Ghislain Viau
Jacket Photograph: Dan De Los Monteros
Photograph of the Author: Joakim Bergström
English translator: Ingrid Lang
Editing: Pamela Guerrieri

To my wife, Gunilla, and our children, Pernilla, John, and Joanna; and our grandchildren, Wilhelm, Wilhma, Alma, Edwin, and Julia.

May your lives be filled with purpose, prosperity, and peace of mind.

CONTENTS

INTRODUCTION

Leaders are a very special breed of people and are found in every field of human endeavor and activity. Over my years of consulting and coaching leaders, I have always been awed and inspired by leaders who want to make a difference. In today's fast moving, fast changing world there is now more than ever a need for strong, secure, and wise leaders to inspire us—to dream, to be involved, and to contribute to a better world.

As I examined leadership, attempting to distill it down to its essential elements, I found that one quality stood out from the rest: Wisdom. With this awareness, in order to be more effective in my work with leaders, I embarked upon an in-depth exploration of wisdom; what it meant, how it was applied, how it was made practical so it could be acted on instead of just reflected upon. What I discovered was that one man, King Solomon, considered by many to be the wisest leader ever, had it all in one place. My task, then, was to present what Solomon knew so that leaders could use Solomon's wisdom to enhance their work and their own lives.

The book that emerged, *The Wisdom of Solomon*, was first published in Sweden in 1994. Over a decade later it is still in popular demand and I feel that there is a tremendous hunger for real wisdom and deeper guidelines about living and working. King Solomon says: *"Without a vision, the people perish."* I think that many of us today are searching for an overarching vision for our existence and a roadmap to get through life in a more fulfilling way.

This English version of the book, *The Wisdom of Leadership*, is a faithful translation of the Swedish original. It focuses on universal principles that have stood the test of time. They are relevant to all, regardless of the culture or background of the reader. They apply to individuals, to families, to private or public organizations of every kind. In the same way that the laws of nature bring order to the universe, these principles direct human co-existence, success, and happiness. When we build our lives and leadership on these principles, we gain insight and become more complete individuals.

It is written that when Solomon was crowned as Israel's king and leader, God appeared to him in a dream, offering that any particular gift would be granted to him. What an opportunity for Solomon to ask for fame, fortune, and a good life for himself. Instead, as stated in II Chronicles 1:10, Solomon says: *"Now give me wisdom and knowledge to properly guide this people."*

Did Solomon lose anything in this? When he asked for wisdom he got so much more. *"For wisdom gives: A long, good life, riches, honor, pleasure, peace"* (Proverb 3:17). The message is that the individual who searches for wisdom will receive inspiration and reward in every aspect of living—which guides each seeker to a rich life, in the truest sense of the word.

The Wisdom of Leadership presents the story of a series of meetings between the Queen of Sheba and King Solomon (described in I Kings 10). The reason for these meetings was that the Queen of Sheba had heard rumors about Solomon's wisdom and successful governing. Spurred by curiosity, she traveled to Jerusalem to meet him in person and learn from his wisdom. During her visit she states (I Kings 10:4), *"Your wisdom and wealth are much greater than anything I have ever heard of."* As the story goes, Solomon becomes a mentor of sorts for the Queen of Sheba.

Their meeting is a biblical episode. My story, on the other hand, is fictitious, structured with instructional guidelines for the reader. People and settings are rendered as faithfully as possible based on my research describing this time period. Many facts are gathered from the Old Testament, especially II Kings. Italicized quotations in the book are from *The Living Bible; a paraphrase.*

Most quotations are borrowed from Proverbs, one of three poetic books in the Old Testament. Proverbs is a book of wisdom with practical, intellectual, and moral purpose. The essence of Proverbs is considered to come from Solomon while some of its content is attributed to other authors. Solomon's proverbs are interwoven with insights and knowledge gleaned from my experience as a leadership consultant.

The proverbs and principles in each chapter will lend support for your own individual reflection and development. It is this individual reflection, or the parts you choose to take with you, that becomes the core of your development. Thus it is advisable to identify the three or four most important insights regarding your personal development after reading each chapter. You may write a lot or just a few lines, but it is important that you save your reflections.

I know it is not usual practice to jot down notes in a book, but I strongly suggest you do so in this one. My experience after many years' work in training and development is that doing this will support you in energizing your inner thoughts and bringing them to action, which will establish for you a practical reality containing deeper values. These are values built on personal reflection, insights, and the wisdom that you choose to embrace.

I do not claim there to be a simple method for development and growth, but as you follow these simple yet powerful principles in your daily life, you will experience an inner source of security, guidance, and wisdom. This will lift you to higher levels in all areas of your life, filling your life with purpose, prosperity, and peace of mind.

Per Winblad
Stockholm

*"Some rich people are poor, and some
poor people have great wealth."*

—King Solomon

1

True Success Comes from Within

She was the picture of beauty. As the caravan slowly pressed onward in the early morning haze, her silhouette appeared against the rising sun. A gold crown adorned her head, with her black hair hanging loosely, covering her shoulders. Her perfectly shaped lips were barely visible through the delicate, white veil. A necklace of gold and carnelian shimmered around her neck, swaying with the gait of the camel and disappearing into her softly rounded bosom. Bracelets circling her wrists jingled. She wore sandals with thin straps and jewels between each toe. Her toenails were painted bright red—a color fit for the queen that she was.

The Queen of Sheba was on her way to Jerusalem to visit King Solomon. Now the city of Jerusalem rose visible on the horizon, like a fortress shaped by nature. It had taken the caravan three years to travel the long road from Sheba in southwest Arabia, through vast deserts and sand dunes in the scorching sun. A large court of assistants and servants traveled with her, tending to her needs. She brought with her to Jerusalem many riches; the camels carried spices, gold, and precious gems as gifts for King Solomon.

The Queen of Sheba ruled over a vast land where people had been engaged in trade and transportation between India and the countries bordering the Mediterranean Sea. The Menoan people and culture had prospered here but were overthrown by the Sabeans. After taking power, the Sabeans governed from the city of Sirwali, located in one of the most desolate areas of Arabia. When the Queen of Sheba became ruler, a new palace was constructed in the capital city bearing her name. The city was located on a high mountain along the road stretching between Aden and Marib.

One of the camel drivers shouted an order and the caravan come to a halt. It stopped in the forecourt of King Solomon's palace towering before them against a clear blue sky. The palace was built of cedar from Lebanon and surrounded by a looming stonewall. A couple of servants scurried to the queen's side and assisted her to descend from the ornate palanquin on the back of the white camel. With delicate steps the queen was guided onto the dusty earth below, leaving the comfort of her chair, adorned with pillows in gold brocade and a linen roof that protected the queen from the searing heat during the journey. She walked with her escorts through the large gates leading into the palace. A winter garden was located in an impressive courtyard nearby. The garden was draped with linen, cotton, and dark blue cloth, covered with white and red ribbons tied to silver rings on columns of white marble. Gold and silver benches dotted the floor, which displayed inlays of green and white marble and shimmering onyx. The Queen of Sheba moved with the grace befitting a queen, as she continued further into the palace, to the big hall of pillars.

Once inside the hall of pillars, she glanced around. What she saw exceeded all her expectations. Onyx columns lined both sides of the hall, the bottom halves black and the top halves wine-colored with gold squares on top near the ceiling and on the bottom near the floor. The columns supported the gold-shimmering ceiling. Tapestries in varying patterns and colors decorated the walls. In the center of the room was a fountain, surrounded by tall palm trees. Couches upholstered with gold foil were placed on the marble floor with inlays of alabaster, pearls, and precious stones. Fruit bowls in algumwood from Ophir had been placed on tables made from cypress and ivory. A fragrance of apples and ginger lingered throughout the room.

The queen crossed the wide marble floor, past rows of alert guards in shining uniforms, heading toward two great pillars bordering the entrance to the throne room. Her eyes settled on a throne of ivory layered with pure gold. Six steps led upward to the throne seat, where the backrest curved around the back. The seat had two armrests with a lion standing at attention by each one. Another twelve lions stood uniformly on the six steps, one on each side.

King Solomon sat on the throne, dressed in royal blue and white robes. He wore a cloak of white and purple over the robes. A simple gold necklace hung around his neck and on his head glittered his crown, the hailed symbol of kingship. His wavy hair was jet black showcasing his youth, and his calm and deep-set eyes appeared to penetrate right through her. His hands rested calmly on the armrests of his throne.

Solomon, the King of Israel, inherited the throne from his father David. He governed successfully and had realized the dream of a powerful and flourishing Israel. Trade and traffic abounded, and craftsmen were busy with large construction projects around the country. Building the Temple and Solomon's palace alone required seventy thousand carpenters, eighty thousand stonemasons, and three thousand and six hundred foremen.

Solomon's empire included all lands west of the Euphrates river, from Tifsa to Gaza, and further from the land of the Philistines to the Egyptian border. The country was at peace with its neighbors mainly because of King Solomon's ability to create and maintain good neighborly relationships. The people felt safe and each family owned a home and garden. Every month the tax collectors provided Solomon and his court with food and any other necessities. They were also responsible for providing the royal stables with special feed for the king's four thousand carriage horses and twelve thousand riding mounts.

Solomon was renowned for his great wisdom and intellect; his knowledge seemed boundless. Yes, his wisdom was much greater than that of the wise men in the East and in Egypt. Rumors of his wisdom spread to the surrounding countries and several kings sent their ambassadors to Solomon for advice. They all brought gifts, items of silver and gold, beautiful cloth, incense, spices, horses, and mules. This continued year after year.

Now the Queen of Sheba stood before King Solomon with the same driving intrigue to know the depths of his wisdom. Two of his closest men accompanied her as she approached him. He rose from his throne and greeted her in the customary manner. After welcoming the Queen of Sheba, King Solomon escorted her to the end of the throne room, where they sat down on a pair of divans. The queen turned to King Solomon and said, "I have heard that you are greater than any other king on earth, both in wealth and in wisdom. I have traveled the long road from Sheba to meet you in person. I have also brought a few gifts with me from my own country."

As she said this, she raised her arm and made a subtle gesture with her hand. Her servant immediately hurried to her side and presented the king with gold, precious stones, and a great variety of aromatic spices. King Solomon thanked her for the wonderful gifts and the Queen of Sheba continued: "I have been told that you have written hundreds of wise proverbs."

She paused and looked at Solomon who leaned forward, signaling for her to continue. "I have long searched for the answer to a most important question without finding it. Now my hope is that you in your wisdom will be able to help me. Tell me, what are the secrets behind a successful life?"

King Solomon thought about her inquiry for a moment, and then leaned back, put his hands together, and said, "I feel honored that you have come all the way from Sheba to visit me. I also feel honored that you ascribe such great wisdom to me. But I am afraid the rumor of my wisdom is considerably exaggerated. I wish my father David were still alive to tell you the principles of success. He was an excellent example of a successful person and would have been better able to answer your question. A simple shepherd from the beginning, without any obvious opportunities to succeed, he eventually became the King of Israel. My father achieved many impressive heroic deeds and overcame significant difficulties. Already as a very young man he defeated the giant warrior Goliath with a mere slingshot and a few stones. Regarding my own accomplishments, they only consist of continuing the work that my father David started. To be honest, I do not know if I am the best person to answer such a deep question."

After listening to King Solomon's words, the Queen of Sheba spoke. "It is difficult for me to believe, after the rumors I have heard about you and your wisdom, that it should not contain a great deal of truth. As I told you, I have traveled a long way to hear your wisdom and I am eager to learn." Her voice grew quiet as her eyes eagerly sought King Solomon's.

Solomon smiled and said, "Your determination and persistence demonstrate your integrity." He paused and then continued, "I am willing to visit with you each day and try to answer your questions. It is important that you spend some time after each conversation reflecting on that which may contribute to your own development. You have already brought up one of the most important conditions for living a successful life: that we are open and eager to learn. But we also have to put what we learn into practice. Because it is only with action that something is accomplished. A wise man once said, 'We forget what we hear, we remember what we see, but only what we do will remain.' Do you agree that my requirements for sharing my wisdom are reasonable?" he asked.

> We forget what we hear, we remember what we see, but only what we do will remain.

The Queen of Sheba replied, "I appreciate your hospitality and your offer to support me in my quest. I will do everything I can to seek to understand and learn. I will also do my best to turn what I learn into action."

"So we are in agreement," King Solomon concluded with a nod. Smiling, he continued, "Then we better get started at once."

He leaned in toward his eager pupil. "Some of the principles I am about to share with you may seem simple and basic at first, as they are founded on wisdom and common sense. However, I still want to encourage you to realize their value. *Guard my words as your most precious possession. Write them down, and also keep them deep within your heart.*"

Solomon continued. "Legend tells of a people that were corrupted and sinful. They had abandoned all wisdom. So the Father of Wisdom decided to hide the secret of success and happiness where it never again would be found. But where should he hide the secret? He decided to summon his counselors and discuss the matter.

"When the counselors were gathered, one of them said, 'Let us hide the secret of happiness and success deep, deep down in the ground.' But the Father of Wisdom answered, 'No, this will not work because men will dig deep and find the secret.'

"Another counselor suggested, 'Let us sink the secret in the deepest ocean.'

"But again, the Father of Wisdom disagreed. 'Man will dive deep into the ocean and find the secret.'

"Another man said, 'Let us hide it on top of the highest mountain there is.' But yet again the Father of Wisdom rejected this proposal. 'Man will surely climb the mountain, find the secret, and take it with him.'

"So the counselors said, 'We give up. There is no place, neither on land nor at sea, where we can hide the secret to happiness and success so man will not find it.'

"But then the Father of Wisdom said, 'This is what we will do. Let us hide the secret to happiness and success deep within man, because that is one place where he will never think of looking.'

"And to this day, according to the legend, man has chased and searched the world over. But all the digging, all the diving, and all the climbing have been in vain—for the secret resided within each person the whole time."

King Solomon's voice trailed off as the Queen of Sheba listened in wonder. All was quiet for a moment before he continued, his voice resonating against the massive walls, "I think all people want to live a successful life, but few have really considered what it entails. Sadly enough, most people equate success with wealth, power, and fame. But let me ask you: Is he who becomes wealthy but loses his family or his health successful? Is he who uses power for the sake of his own winnings successful? Is he who wins the whole world but loses himself successful? No. Wealth, power, and fame do not guarantee contentment or success. It is better to allow the experiences we consider meaningful to lead us. To look for love and to be loved—and the most important of all: to find inner peace of mind.

"*Some rich people are poor, and some poor people have great wealth.* If we want to live a rich and fulfilling life, we need to realize that true success comes from within. It cannot be acquired or achieved. It is not a destiny we reach someday, thus molding us into successful people. It is a journey we travel our whole lives long. It is knowing one's

"Some rich people are poor, and some poor people have great wealth."

purpose in life and achieving a balance within each important aspect of our lives. To continue to grow emotionally, socially, intellectually, financially, and spiritually while contributing to the growth of others.

"*The rich man thinks of his wealth as an impregnable defense, a high wall of safety. What a dreamer!* There is nothing wrong with being rich; money is neither good nor evil. It is our attitude toward money and the way we spend it that is important. Money is a good servant but a poor master. Money must therefore be managed mindfully and spent for greater purposes. Wealth and what it brings are like power and fame, fleeting commodities, which may quickly disappear.

"*Only wisdom brings a meaningful life, and only he who holds on to this becomes happy.*"

"*Only wisdom brings a meaningful life, and only he who holds on to this becomes happy.* Wisdom offers what wealth, power, and fame cannot give. Being rich is not about money; it's about inner, deeper values such as meaning, contentment, happiness, and peace of mind. To be wise we need to reflect upon what is most important to us in life and what has less meaning. We need to put our lives into perspective and find out who we are, where we want to go, and what kind of persons and leaders we want to become during our journey.

"For wisdom and truth will enter the very center of your being, filling your life with joy. Wisdom will guide you to a rich and good life; it helps us discover what is truly meaningful to us in a broader view of life. Wisdom also signifies the ability to separate real joy from temporary happiness. When we possess wisdom and truth at the very center of our beings, it will surely fill our lives with joy while we grow and develop as human beings.

"When you enjoy becoming wise, there is hope for you! A bright future lies ahead! As we enjoy becoming wise, asking important questions, learning from our experiences in life, and seeking truth in all we do, we learn, grow, and mature. Wisdom helps us apply our knowledge in the best possible way. It indicates insight, common sense, and sound judgment. And consider this: *A wise man is mightier than a strong man. Wisdom is mightier than strength.*

> *"A wise man is mightier than a strong man. Wisdom is mightier than strength."*

"Happy is the man who is so anxious to be with me [wisdom] that he watches for me daily at my gates, or waits for me outside my home. Many opportunities open up every day for those who eagerly search for wisdom. Every day each person and each encounter can teach us something of value.

"Determination to be wise is the first step toward becoming wise! At the very moment we make the decision to want to

"For wisdom gives: A long, good life, riches, honor, pleasure, peace. "

be wise, a chain of actions begins to unfold. We can make that decision right now. It is an individual choice because we have a free will of our own. With the first step behind us, we are on our way to a better future. We will be lifted to new and higher levels in every aspect of our lives. *For wisdom gives: A long, good life, riches, honor, pleasure, peace."*

King Solomon observed the Queen of Sheba in wait of her reaction. "Indeed, your insight stems from the well of wisdom and has given me much to contemplate," she said, adding, "I am already looking forward to continuing our conversation another day, as I understand you have many duties. Tell me, what do you want me to do in the meantime?"

King Solomon answered, "I would like you to spend the afternoon considering the following questions:

What does real success mean to you?

What drives you forward?

What gives you joy and fulfillment?

How do you balance what drives you and what gives you joy and fulfillment?"

The following morning as the first rays of sunlight filtered through the palms and the garnet apple trees, the Queen of Sheba arrived for her next visit with King Solomon. The air teemed with fragrance and the grass still harbored drops of morning dew as she padded through the palace gates. King Solomon, this day dressed in a white and purple mantle, smiled warmly and beckoned her to sit by his throne. He ordered the two guards who stood always by his side to retreat, leaving only the specially chosen servants. They fanned their down-white feathers to offer some relief from the heat in the room.

After a discussion about the long journey from Sheba to Jerusalem, Solomon asked the queen whether she and her entourage had been well cared for, which she confirmed.

He continued by asking, "Have you had the opportunity to consider what we discussed yesterday and search for answers to my questions? And most important, what have you decided to do?"

The queen answered, "I have reflected much on your words and considered your questions. First now I am beginning to understand what true success is all about. That what drives me is not always the same as what gives me joy and fulfillment. In my daily aspiration for wealth and power, I have neglected what truly gives me joy and fulfillment. I have not spent enough time with my family and my closest friends. I have not taken the time to walk in my beautiful gardens with the pistachio trees and fragrant almond blossoms. I have not taken the time to reflect and learn from my experience. I have not even taken the time for my daily prayers of thankfulness because of my eagerness and ambition. In this way I have reflected over your questions and decided on the following:

"From now on I will regularly take time to be alone with myself for receptive silence and reflection. This will help me to see the bigger and longer perspective of my life. I now realize that true success and happiness only can come from within. Success in the form of money, power, and prestige may give me many dishes on the dinner table but no appetite; beautiful clothes but not beauty; an impressive house but not necessarily a happy home. Therefore, I will attempt to create harmony between what drives me, my tangible successes, and what gives me inner joy and fulfillment.

"From now on I will consider each new day as a precious gift. Every hour, minute, and second offer something great to experience. I will strive to enjoy the fruits of my work in the company of those I love, my family and loved ones. I will experience the greatness of nature and seize the beauty of the moment by basking in my gardens, enjoying nature as the leaves change color. I will stroll along the beach and watch the sun slowly disappear in the sea.

"From now on I will try to learn something from everything I experience and everyone I meet. I will always try to gain knowledge and wisdom so that I can contribute to the development of others and of society as a whole. Then I can face each day with confidence, joy, and inner peace."

My Own Reflections

*"Be careful how you think;
your life is shaped by your thoughts."*
—King Solomon

2

Your Thoughts Shape Your Life

Late afternoon that same day, the Queen of Sheba arrived for another visit with King Solomon. He greeted her as he put away his golden scepter, rose from his throne, and asked the queen to accompany him on a tour of the palace and its grounds. He walked down the six steps and continued across the marble floor. The clatter from their sandals echoed between the onyx columns as they approached a narrow arched opening in the wall. The opening was not easily detected in the flickering light of the oil lamps, but immediately inside the musty darkness a stairway wound its way upward, leading to the dome of the palace.

When they reached the top of the steep stairway, they were both out of breath from the effort. They stopped to catch their breath before continuing to the nearest room, named the Lebanon Forest Hall. Heavy beams of cedar rested on four rows of cedar columns. The hall was empty except for a long table composed of citrus wood surrounded by twelve high-backed chairs. Ornamental palm leaves and flowers decorated the backs of the chairs. Along the walls were two hundred long shields and three hundred round shields of hammered gold. The walls seemed alive as the sunlight reflected off the hammered surfaces of the shields. Forty-five windows in three rows surrounded the hall.

The view was splendid with King Solomon's Temple in the foreground. The Temple was built by Tyrean artists and builders on top of Moria Mountain. To the west were vineyards, flourishing gardens, and blooming parks. To the south, they enjoyed a panoramic view of the huge reservoirs that stored water to irrigate the plantations. To the east were the horse stables, and scattered amongst the lush green surroundings were a multitude of storage sheds and other buildings. All of this was part of Solomon's construction program.

They entered the balcony that surrounded the hall and lingered there, letting the fresh air fill their lungs. Solomon pointed to the stables and explained that he was a collector of carriages and riding horses. The carriages were brought in from Egypt and royal tradesmen imported the horses from Musri and Kuve. He now owned one thousand four hundred carriages and twelve thousand horses, located in specific cities as well as in the king's palace in Jerusalem.

After showing all this, Solomon became quiet for a moment and then said, "Let me now continue to answer your question about the right principles for a successful life."

"If we want true success in life, we need to realize
that our thoughts shape our lives and our future."

*"Be careful how you think; your life is shaped by your
thoughts.* Our thoughts are powerful. They direct our actions
and shape our lives and our futures.
Whatever we dwell upon and think
about grows and expands in our individual lives. Our thoughts are like
seeds in a garden. What we plant today
will grow tomorrow. If we plant roses,
we reap roses. If we plant weeds, we
will reap weeds. Our thoughts are
like a double-edged sword. They may
lead us to a healthy life filled with
happiness and prosperity, or to a life
of misery and suffering.

> Whatever we
> dwell upon and
> think about grows
> and expands in
> our individual lives.

*"The wicked man's fears will all come true, and so will
the good man's hopes.* When we concentrate our thinking
on the good things we would like to see happen in every
situation, we move ahead in the direction we desire. The
opposite is concentrating on what we do not want to happen.
Thinking on the possibilities moves our focus from 'What
is wrong?' to 'How do we want it to be? When we search
for a more positive view upon every situation offered us in
life, all our hopes will come true.'

*"When a man is gloomy, everything seems to go wrong;
when he is cheerful, everything seems right!* Our thoughts also

"When a man is gloomy, everything seems to go wrong; when he is cheerful, everything seems right!"

control our feelings. We do not feel negative or downcast by accident. It is our reaction to what happens to us, the manner in which we think, that is crucial. If we think unhappy thoughts we will feel unhappy, and if we think happy thoughts we will feel happy. Decide how you will think and in turn you will decide how you will feel. Perhaps you have heard the expression: Where there is life, there is hope. It would be more correct to say: Where there is hope, there is life.

"A wise man's heart leads him to do right, and a fool's heart leads him to do evil. It is possible to guide our thoughts in the right direction if we guard them. But changing the way we think does not happen overnight. Our negative thoughts will not suddenly disappear, unlike the morning dew that evaporates in the heat of the sun. It takes time, patience, and practice. When we find ourselves thinking negatively, we stop and ask ourselves what the exact opposite would be. Then we begin to think about that, letting the positive thought take over. Learning and practicing possibility thinking requires self-discipline, but it is worth the effort for it will promote inner strength, which in turn gives us power and energy. Like a king has the power to reign over his kingdom, we have the power to rule over our thoughts.

"A cheerful heart does good like medicine, but a broken spirit makes one sick. One condition for an active and healthy life is to look at the bright side. We feel better and live longer. A person with a happy heart radiates a sense of well-being and health, which spreads to those around him. Like a bird arouses other birds by its chirping until all the birds are singing in a wonderful choir, one positive thought stimulates other positive thoughts to life and energy.

"Only a simpleton believes what he is told! A prudent man checks to see where he is going. A wise man is cautious and avoids danger; a fool plunges ahead with great confidence. Being a possibility thinker is not the same as living in the clouds naively believing everything will turn out fine. It does not mean claiming that everything is wonderful when things are not. Problems that are ignored soon turn into crises. To be a possibility thinker is to see a situation the

"Only a simpleton believes what he is told! A prudent man checks to see where he is going."

way it is and do something about it—to seek support and find the pearls of wisdom needed to move forward.

"A prudent man foresees the difficulties ahead and prepares for them; the simpleton goes blindly on and suffers the consequences. We all encounter situations we consider difficult or problematic, because that is life. Changes occur continually. Change equals development. We also change

as persons continually. We grow older, not younger. We encounter highs and lows, stormy nights and sunny days. Life is like the seasons. During the freezing cold winter everything seems dark and impossible. Spring arrives with new possibilities, and we must sow if we plan to harvest in the fall. Summer is filled with work and heat from the sun, and we must protect and care for our garden to enjoy a good harvest. In the fall, we harvest the products of our work and welcome the colorful dusk of the season. By accepting change as a natural part of life, we take important steps toward personal development.

"It is dangerous and sinful to rush into the unknown. A man may ruin his chances by his own foolishness and then blame it on the Lord! We must face the risk of failure in order to be successful. But this is not the same as rushing into the unknown. We must carefully consider and weigh the consequences and make sensible decisions. He who wants to be successful takes calculated risks."

King Solomon observed the Queen of Sheba, noting her wide-eyed interest, and continued, "To conclude, let me ask you a few questions. Are you a possibility-thinker or a problem-thinker? Do you direct your thoughts toward the things you want to achieve rather than toward the things you want to avoid? What would your life be like if it was exactly the way you hoped for?"

With Solomon's words still clear in her ears, the Queen of Sheba returned to her luxurious suite near the palace. She was dazed by the intensity she felt in Solomon's presence. As she ambled through the long hallway, she reflected on her own style of reasoning in various circumstances and was amazed at what Solomon said about the power of one's thoughts.

She entered the peaceful suite and lowered herself on a cluster of soft pillows decorated with gold embroidery and sequins mimicking the rising sun over the mountains. Soon a servant entered the room and told her a warm bath had been prepared for her. The servant gently untied the straps of the queen's thin silk clothing, which fell to the floor. She removed the necklace of gold links with silver spheres and the thin gold chain around her wrist. The jewelry was placed in a wooden box covered with pearls and shells. The servant bathed the Queen of Sheba in warm, perfumed water and massaged her body with fragrant oils. The queen went to bed between colored sheets of the finest Egyptian linen with a faint scent of myrrh, aloe, and cinnamon. She immediately fell asleep like a weary child as the burnt red sunset behind the gardens sliced through the windows, casting a pink hue throughout the entire room.

The following morning, the queen awoke early to the sound of birds and the scents from the flowering garden. The sun was slowly rising over the Temple and cast shadows of the roof-ridge on the mountainside. She spent the first thirty minutes relaxing, breathing in the fresh air, and listening to the sounds of nature. A new day, a miracle, a life in miniature never to return, to spend in the best way possible. The rest of the morning, she thought about Solomon's questions.

The queen appeared at the palace at the time agreed upon and was immediately escorted to the place of honor beside King Solomon. He was involved in conversation with the elders who were seated in a balcony of cedar on the right side of the throne. Below the throne, a monkey scampered back and forth waving feathers, accompanied by laughter and chuckles of those gathered. The servants, whose job it was to fan the air with their ostrich feathers, tried to remain composed but were hardly successful.

King Solomon turned to the Queen of Sheba and said, "I hope everything is to your satisfaction concerning your stay in my palace."

The Queen of Sheba assured him that neither her escorts nor herself had ever been treated better. Then she said, "I am prepared to answer your questions and have come to the following conclusions today:

"From now on I will be aware that my thoughts shape my life and my future. I will concentrate my thoughts toward the things I want to achieve and in the direction I desire for my life. I am the crown of creation and am able to realize my dreams by believing in myself and my abilities. My decisions and actions decide my future, not my circumstances! I will spend time each morning creating a picture of my day and also time each week creating a picture of my future in a bigger, long-term perspective.

"From now on I will dwell on the good things about my life and try to see things from the brighter side. With a joyful heart, I will radiate well-being, which will rub off on people around me. A gold coin has two sides and so do people, places, and work—a good side and a bad side. I will choose to look for the good sides and strive to see opportunities where I previously saw problems.

"From now on I will remember that my thoughts are like a seed in my garden. What I sow today, I will reap tomorrow. My thoughts can lead me to a life filled with happiness, prosperity, and health. Sowing positive thoughts will bring a harvest of an inner state of faith, hope, and trust …"

———————

My Own Reflections

Your Thoughts Shape Your Life

"The swiftest person does not always win the race, nor the strongest man the battle. Wise men are often poor, and skillful men are not necessarily famous."

—King Solomon

3

Let Adversity and Struggle Give You Strength

The next morning, the Queen of Sheba smiled to herself as she entered the throne room. "Today I will really test Solomon's wisdom," she thought to herself.

She carried two beautiful bouquets filled with red lilies, yellow lotus flowers, and white hanging flowers from a sycamore tree. One bouquet was made from fresh flowers, the other from artificial flowers. However, the artificial bouquet was so skillfully made that no one could tell the difference, not even by the fragrance.

The guards bowed and stepped aside. She entered the throne room where Solomon waited, stopped a few steps from him, and said, "Tell me, King Solomon, may I ask you a question?" Solomon nodded his agreement and she continued, "Which of these bouquets consists of fresh-cut flowers, and which consists of artificial flowers?"

Solomon thought carefully, with his chin in his hand, then said, "Give me a moment to think about your question, and please open the window to let some air in." The queen opened the window and the room was filled with scents from the garden and the sound of birds chirping. A bee suddenly flew in through the window and began circling the bouquets of flowers. Eventually the bee landed on the bouquet of fresh flowers and the king pointed and exclaimed, "Those are the real flowers."

The Queen of Sheba was amazed and asked, "How did you know this would happen when I opened the window?"

Solomon replied, "Only fresh flowers attract interest and attention. Artificial flowers lack an inner life, although they do look fresh on the outside." He continued, "This is also the case with people. Only those who are vital and genuine become successful. And above all, one must be true to oneself."

"Tell me, where does your wisdom come from?" the queen asked.

Once again, Solomon contemplated this in silence before he answered. "I do not develop any really great ideas from my own observations or my own conclusions. I do not make any really big discoveries through my own research. I receive wisdom from the great mystery, which sometimes comes to us in our dreams. I have learned to take my dreams seriously. Dreams are like a mirror of our inner selves. Our dreams see further than our eyes. The light flows in and reveals our inner secrets. It is important to remain open to what our inner voice tells us."

Solomon continued, "In our culture, dreams have always been of importance. It is said that Pharaoh dreamed he was standing on the bank of the River Nile when suddenly seven healthy, fat cows rose up from the river and began grazing along the riverbank. Soon seven more cows arose from the river, bony enough to count their ribs. They lined up beside the fat cows and proceeded to eat them!

"The dream made Pharaoh confused and upset. He continued to dream, this time of seven heads of grain and every grain was well-rounded and ample. Suddenly, the stalk grew more grains, which soon shriveled and became scorched by the easterly wind. Once again, these meager grains swallowed the ample, full grains!

"Then Pharaoh called for a man named Joseph, an interpreter of dreams. Pharaoh sought the meaning of the dreams and Joseph answered him, saying, 'Both dreams mean the same thing. God has shown you his plans for Egypt. The next seven years well be a period of prosperity in all of Egypt. But following this will be seven years of famine. The famine will be so horrible that even the memory of the good years will vanish.'

"Pharaoh cried out in anguish, 'This is terrible! What should I do?'

"Joseph replied, 'I suggest you find the wisest man in Egypt and put him in charge of an agricultural program. I suggest you divide Egypt into five administrative areas and let those responsible for each area gather any excess crops in the royal storage buildings during the next seven years in order to have enough food when the famine comes. Otherwise, disaster will strike the country.'

"Heeding Joseph's advice, Pharaoh selected Joseph as head of the agricultural project and he was given Pharaoh's own signet ring as proof of his authority. Pharaoh dressed him in beautiful clothes and placed a royal gold chain around his neck, and exclaimed, 'Look, this is the man I have appointed as responsible for the entire land of Egypt.'

"The following seven years brought great harvests everywhere, and Joseph collected part of all the harvests for the government, storing them in the cities. After seven years of successful work, the storage buildings were filled and the grain was plentiful beyond measure. Finally, the seven good years came to an end and seven years of famine began, just as Joseph had predicted. And the harvests failed in Egypt and the countries surrounding it. At this time Joseph opened the doors to the stored grain when the severe famine spread around the world. There was not only enough food for the Egyptians, but also enough to help those who came to Egypt from other countries to purchase grain."

Solomon finished his story and concluded, "Now you see what the unknown within you, who I know is the voice of God, may do for those who listen."

The Queen of Sheba had listened intently and now spoke, her voice awe-filled, "Your advice and wisdom are surely worth more than gold and silver."

Solomon accepted the compliment with a smile and continued, "Now let us continue with your question about the right principles for a successful life."

> "If we want true success in life, we need to let adversity and struggle give us strength."

"Let us rejoice when we encounter adversity and struggles because we know they are good for us. What kind of people would we be if we never encountered difficulties? Lifting heavy burdens makes us stronger. Courage comes from the moment of fear. Problems make us humble and wise. Through suffering we learn patience and inner strength, and character results from patience."

Solomon gestured to the open window. "The strongest cedar tree in Lebanon's forests has not been protected from the wind or the sun's burning rays. It grew in the open, enduring storms, rain, and shine, plunging its roots deep into the soil. Now it is firmly planted and the birds are building their nests high above the ground.

Lifting heavy burdens makes us stronger. Courage comes from the moment of fear. Problems make us humble and wise.

"We cannot always choose what will happen to us in life, but we can choose how it will affect us. Temporary obstacles and disappointments are part of life; they are inevitable.

Everything does not always work out the way we plan or hope. The arrow does not hit its target every time. Trials and disappointments usually affect us in one of two ways: we may grow from them or we may become discouraged.

"How we react to life's experiences determines whether we will live a successful life or not. Failures are nothing but life's way of teaching. This does not mean that we have not accomplished anything, just that we have more to learn.

"The only people who never fail are those who never try. It is impossible to win a race if we do not show up at the start line, impossible to win if we do not dare to compete. We will never know what we may achieve if we never try. But with each try, there is a risk of failure and disappointment. Still, we must dare to fail, if we are ever to succeed. How sad it is when a person does not reach his full potential because he fears failure. It is better to try and fail than to not try at all.

"A man who refuses to admit his mistakes can never be successful. But if he confesses and forsakes them, he gets another chance." Failures help us understand our weaknesses and enable us to overcome them. Even if it sounds strange, we learn more from our failures than from our

> *"A man who refuses to admit his mistakes can never be successful. But if he confesses and forsakes them, he gets another chance."*

44

successes. We analyze what went wrong and use the knowledge for further development. We make new decisions, start over, and try again.

"But we must not dwell too long on our mistakes or be too hard on ourselves. Disappointments can easily turn into bitterness. There is nothing we can do to change the past. We may make some bad choices, but we also may make some good choices. What is important is to concentrate on what we did right, remember it, and apply it to the future. There is always another chance. When God closes a door on us, he will open a window at the same time.

"The intelligent man is always open to new ideas. In fact, he looks for them. It is important to be open and see the positive opportunities in each situation. Each difficulty, setback, or failure carries a seed for a new opportunity. Consider the huge resources that were discovered only through great hardship. In our worst predicaments, new, daring ideas will come to us, and we make the leap to new growth. When we look for opportunities in every setback, the rock we once tripped over becomes a step to new and bigger accomplishments."

> "*The intelligent man is always open to new ideas. In fact, he looks for them.*"

Solomon's teaching again fascinated the Queen of Sheba. She looked at him hopefully and said, "Your wisdom tastes like honey and makes me hungry for more. But tell me, how do you deal with sudden and unfair tragedies? I recall several instances in my court." Suddenly her features changed as sympathy welled up in her eyes. "One of my servants was rejected on her wedding day when the bridegroom-to-be left without a word. Another worker in my court was hit by lightning and lost a leg. How can one deal with such misfortunes and disappointments? Nothing good comes out of it." Her voice begged for an answer.

Solomon considered this for a long time before he answered, saying, "Let me share a story I heard about an old farmer who lived in a small, poor village. He was considered wealthy because he had a son, and he owned the only horse in the village. One day, the horse ran off into the mountains and the villagers consoled the farmer, saying, 'You lost your horse, such bad luck.' The old farmer tugged on his beard and retorted, 'How do you know that this is such a bad luck?'

"Several days later the horse returned accompanied by twelve wild horses. Now the farmer was the owner of not just one, but thirteen horses, and the villagers said, 'How lucky you are!' The old farmer tugged on his beard and replied, 'How do you know that this is luck?'

"One day his son was riding one of the wild horses and was thrown off, breaking both legs and arms. Filled with pity, the villagers said to the farmer, 'What happened to your son is terrible; this time you must certainly agree that you have had bad luck.' The old farmer tugged on his beard and asked them once again, 'How do you know that this is bad luck?'

"Some time later, a warlord came by and took all the healthy men in the village to be sent off to war except the old farmer's son, since he was crippled. And the villagers said, 'Your son is the only one left; how lucky you are!' And the old farmer smiled, his eyes shining as he said, 'How do you know that this is luck?' This time they all laughed together, knowing that the old farmer had been right all along not to quickly judge any situation."

Finishing this story, Solomon looked at the queen and they both burst out laughing. Soon Solomon turned serious again and explained, "It is true that life is not fair. *The swiftest person does not always win the race, nor the strongest man the battle. Wise men are often poor, and skillful men are not necessarily famous.* We are sometimes struck unfairly by losses, which may be heavy to bear. But we have to see life in a longer perspective, always looking upon what we have left—not upon what we have lost!

"Even when we suffer considerable losses, we still have something of value left. We have close friends and other precious relationships. We have gained

> *"The swiftest person does not always win the race, nor the strongest man the battle. Wise men are often poor, and skillful men are not necessarily famous."*

knowledge and wisdom. We have many beautiful memories. More importantly, we have something no loss or no person can take away from us: The freedom and power to choose how we will respond to what happens to us. No matter what has happened, is now happening, or will happen, there is a space between those things and our responses to them. Next to life itself, the power of choice is our greatest gift.

"We choose to respond constructively. We choose to turn the negative into something positive and learn from it. As someone once said: 'Setbacks are inevitable, misery is a choice.'"

Solomon leaned closer to the Queen of Sheba and asked, "Do you remember Joseph whom I told you about earlier?"

"Yes," she replied. "He who helped Pharaoh interpret his dreams and then became responsible for all of Egypt," the queen answered.

"That is correct," replied Solomon. "He is a good example of what I talk about here. Before he became famous in all of Egypt, he had every reason to be discouraged by the difficulties and injustice he encountered in life. I will tell you how it all began.

"Joseph was the son of Jacob, one of Israel's forefathers, and they lived in the land of Canaan. He was the youngest of his many brothers, and was especially dear to his father, since Jacob was rather old when Joseph was born. As Joseph grew up with his brothers, he eventually began to share with them his dreams of someday becoming a man of great importance. This, and the fact that he was favored by their father, made the brothers brood with envy.

"So they plotted against him. When Joseph was seventeen years old, he and his brothers were shepherding Jacob's herds when they came upon several camels and Ishmaelite merchants. Joseph's brothers took the opportunity to sell Joseph as a slave. In an attempt to cover up their evildoings, they told their father that a wild animal had killed him.

"Joseph was again sold by the merchants to Potiphar, who was the master of Pharaoh's bodyguard. In this way, Joseph found himself a servant in a strange house in a foreign country.

"Joseph could have easily become absorbed in bitterness and self-pity, dwelling on all the trouble his brothers had caused him. Instead, he excelled in his work and was promoted to manage not only Potiphar's home, but also his administration and business. Before long, however, he again faced injustice and misfortune.

"One day, he was put in a very difficult situation. Potiphar's wife had taken a liking to the young, handsome Joseph and made advances toward him. Joseph refused to betray Potiphar, and Potiphar's wife became upset at being turned down. In an attempt to grab at him, she tore off Joseph's coat, then called for the guards, showed them the coat, and accused Joseph of assaulting her. When Potiphar arrived home that evening, she recounted the same story to her husband, who became furious and threw Joseph in prison.

"There he remained for thirteen long years, despite his innocence. But even in this difficult situation, he did not become discouraged, but instead tried to make the best of the situation. He soon was entrusted with tasks within the prison, and his reputation and ability to interpret dreams eventually became known to Pharaoh. Joseph was not only pardoned, but became the most important man in the land of Egypt, next to Pharaoh.

"Certainly, we are sometimes struck by injustices in life. But remember! The most important thing is not what happens to us, but how we use our freedom to choose how we respond to those circumstances!

"When we meet adversity and struggles, we shall not ask why this is happening to us. There is no good answer to the question 'why me?' Instead, we should ask ourselves, 'how?' How do we want to respond to this? How can we learn? How can we turn this into something positive?

"Another thing we can do is to consider each misfortune as an opportunity to grow and become a better person, instead of a bitter person. We can lift and inspire others around us, so that when they see our inner strength and our way of turning misfortunes into something constructive, they will be inspired to handle their own situations in the best possible way.

"Sorrow is better than laughter, for sadness has a refining influence on us. Naturally, we must deal with our sorrow and pain by showing our feelings of disappointment; this is natural and necessary. Tears are often a gift from God, and sorrow is a healing emotion; but remember that it is in our power to write a happy ending to the story. After grieving and healing for some time, we can decide to choose

a positive reaction. In this way we rise above our circumstances and are able to carry on … often finding something of personal value in the experience.

"Don't you know that this good man, though you trip him up seven times, will each time rise again? Difficulties will pass. Life goes on. The storm does not last forever and after the rain comes sunshine. Each mountain has its peak. It is not the number of times we stumble and fall that determines whether we reach the peak or not. The deciding factor is how many times we get up and continue climbing."

"Don't you know that this good man, though you trip him up seven times, will each time rise again?"

Solomon grew quiet and then asked the Queen of Sheba: "What have adversities in your life meant to you? What have you learned from them? Would you rather be without these experiences? What is it that you most of all would like to do, considering this fresh insight you have found today?"

Once dismissed from the throne room, the queen chose to take a leisurely walk in the garden after the visit with Solomon. The sun appeared like a burning ball sinking behind the rooftops of the palace. She enjoyed the clean, cool air and sat down in the grass, in the shade of cedar trees and cypresses, and reflected on Solomon's words. Hearing all this wisdom filled her heart with joy. The only thing that troubled her was the feeling of passion she felt after each visit with Solomon.

The sun soon descended into the horizon, and dusk fell. The garden lay warm and still in the darkness, but inside the palace lamps spread a soft light and the breeze brought her nose the scent of food cooking. She could hear the sound of quick footsteps as the servants hurried along the corridors. She decided to go inside and end the day with her usual bath and prepare for the next day in Solomon's company.

The following morning, when the Queen of Sheba arrived in Solomon's quarters, she was surprised and disappointed to find that the king had canceled their meting as a Syrian king unexpectedly paid him a visit. Then she reminded herself: "What did Solomon just tell me? He who wants to be successful chooses to see an opportunity in every setback. I will consider this as an opportunity to visit Jerusalem once more. I will visit the market and look for something to purchase for my family as a memory from my journey."

When the Queen of Sheba returned from her visit to Jerusalem, the sun had lost some of its heat but still shone bright and clear from an almost cloudless sky. The day in Jerusalem had passed quickly and she had been able to purchase many gifts for her family and closest friends. She would bring back with her fine linen from Egypt; exquisite perfumes with nardus, saffron, and calamus; tiny boxes with inlays of electrum, the particular blend of silver and gold that she liked so well; fans in many colors; and much more. The merchants were ecstatic, as the queen had purchased one item after the other and her servants were loaded with goods on their way home.

Once inside her suite she sat down to catch her breath. Shopping in the bazaars was not effortless, and weariness overcame her. Before allowing herself to rest, she once again went through her notes from the previous day:

"From now on I will let adversity and struggle give me strength. I will regard life's journey as a continual period of development. It is my duty to manage and creatively solve all situations offered in life. I will not be discouraged, but instead I will regard misfortunes as information about how far I have come on my journey. This way, I will gather new strength in anticipation of the next phase. Trials will give me the opportunity to learn and grow and will bring out the best in me. Suffering teaches me patience, and my inner strength and character will come from patience.

"From now on I will accept life as it is. I will try to balance what I receive against what I expect, and maintain forward progress. I now realize that my most important asset in life is my freedom to choose my own reaction to what happens to me. I will choose to look upon what I have—not what I have lost! I will choose to learn from mistakes and see the possibility for good that lies in every situation! This way, the stones I have stumbled upon become my steps to development.

"From now on, during difficult periods I will focus on the present and set concrete goals. Each day, step by step, I will manage the various situations that I face. Small but important daily victories will give me positive energy to continue, and will stimulate me to more powerful efforts. Great acts are made of small deeds. This way, I will gather strength to see future situations as opportunities, always being content and thankful for what I already have."

My Own Reflections

"Without vision, the people perish."
—King Solomon

4

Clarify the Vision for Your Desired Future!

Surrounded by her servants, the Queen of Sheba walked through the garden on her way to yet another meeting with King Solomon. Streamers atop flag posts on both sides of the gate flapped in the breeze. In the background, she could hear the sounds of the bazaar—street merchants haggling with shoppers, livestock braying or crowing, children laughing. Suddenly, strong voices rose above the din of the street.

Two women, dressed in linen garments and wearing dangling silver earrings, separated from the crowd. They walked briskly through the gate into the garden. Their nardus and saffron perfume wafted in the air behind them.

"We must speak to the king," demanded one of the women.

"He will decide in this matter," added the other. One of them carried a baby in her arms, clutching it protectively to her body. The child's tiny, high-pitched cry cut through the air.

The scene caught the Queen of Sheba by surprise. She stepped into the shade of the decorative palm leaves, and remained standing in the pillar hall just next to the entrance to the throne room. The women had reached the entry, but here the guards stopped them.

"We must see the king," shouted the woman who held the baby.

"I demand justice," shouted the other.

King Solomon sat on his throne, observing the ruckus. One of the women said, "She stole my baby!" while the other woman interrupted, "No, she stole my baby!"

"Stop!" demanded Solomon. "Come here and tell me what happened, one at a time."

The guards parted to admit the women. "Listen, your majesty," said the one who came empty-handed. "We live in the same house, that woman and I, and that is where I gave birth to a baby boy. Two days later, she also gave birth to a baby boy.

"Her baby died during the night when she happened to lay on top of it. But she is deceitful as well as clumsy, and so she got up in the middle of the night when I was sleeping and took my son, putting her dead son in his place! When I awakened to feed my son in the morning, I saw that he was not the baby I gave birth to, but her dead baby instead."

The other woman shouted, "It is my son who is alive and your son who is dead!"

And the first one cried, "Liar! Your son is dead and mine is alive!" In this manner they carried on in front of the king. Until suddenly they fell silent when Solomon spoke.

"Now let us figure this out," he said. "You both claim that the living child is yours and that the dead baby belongs to the other, correct? And you have no witnesses to verify either of your stories?" The women nodded sullenly. Solomon thought for a moment and then turned sharply to look at the anxious women.

"I know how we shall resolve this, so you are both fairly treated. Guards, come here." Both guards approached and stood on either side of the two women. Solomon bade the woman to give him the child, and she handed it over after a moment's hesitation. Solomon gave the child to one of the guards and told the other, "Now draw your sword and cut the living baby in two. Each woman shall have one half of the child." Solomon sat back and inspected his fingernails, waiting with apparent indifference.

"No!" screamed the woman who really was the mother of the child, and who loved him very much. "Please," she sobbed. "Please don't do this. Let her have the baby instead. Let the baby live!"

But the other woman seethed, "All right, it will be neither yours or mine; divide it between us!"

Then Solomon's face brightened and he declared, "Give the baby to the woman who wants him to live, for she is the mother!"

The baby's mother cradled the child and wept with joy, and the other stalked out angrily. When the women were gone, the Queen of Sheba came forward. Solomon welcomed her and bid her to sit down.

"I could not help but hear your conversation with the two women," she said. "Your wisdom really is as great as I was told."

But Solomon seemed to barely listen. He stared thoughtfully out into the garden. Finally he spoke, "Only the compassionate and unselfish person can set aside her own desires and do what is best for another person. This is what makes a true human being—and a leader."

He turned to the queen and apologized, "Forgive me, I was thinking aloud." They spoke for a while about the bizarre incident with the baby, and then their conversation returned to the queen's thoughts about their last meeting. Solomon continued his explanation of the right principles for a successful life.

> "If we want true success in life, we need to clarify the vision for our desired future and pursue it with passion and discipline!"

"Without a vision, the people perish."

"*Without a vision, the people perish*. We all need a vision for our lives. Vision is holding in our mind's eye a clear picture of a desired and preferred future. We seek something important to strive for and be inspired by; to accomplish something worthwhile. When we have no vision, we lose direction and faith in our future. With a clear picture of the future, something that inspires and captures the heart, it helps us to concentrate our energy on what we most desire.

"*A wise man thinks ahead.* All things are created twice: first inside in our thinking, and then outside in our doing. When we dream of the future and establish goals and plans, we are making the first creation. When we are putting the dreams, goals, and plans into action we are making the second creation."

We seek something important to strive for and be inspired by; to accomplish something worthwhile.

A puzzled expression crossed the queen's brow.

Solomon continued with an illustration: "Imagine that you were to build a palace. You would need to determine how much of the various building materials to purchase. Shiploads of cedar, cypress, and algumwood from Lebanon's forests. You would also have to locate and hire experienced professionals: foremen, carpenters, brickmakers, stone-masons, goldsmiths, and weavers. Now imagine that you are standing on the construction site and all the building material and workers are on site. You order them to start working. The first question the foremen will ask you is: 'Where is the plan? We cannot build a beautiful palace without a drawing or a plan.' Even the most experienced contractor needs a plan. He cannot use his talent effectively without a plan. With a detailed plan, even a less experienced builder can construct a grand palace. But without a plan this would be impossible.

"This is also the case when a person builds a successful life. You are both the architect and the builder. Your life is your construction site. You will be able to build a life filled with happiness and success by having a vision, setting goals, and developing a plan to reach these goals. Only after that can you put it all into action.

"Plans go wrong with too few counselors; many counselors bring success. "

"*Plans go wrong with too few counselors; many counselors bring success.* We all need help and support along the way. As we set goals and plan for our future, we take advice from others. Asking someone for advice is the best compliment we can give that person. It shows respect and faith in his or her judgment. We select our advisors with great care. Even when we have gathered information and listened to the advice and opinions of others, it is still up to us to make the final decision.

"*Be with wise men and become wise.* We begin to resemble those with whom we spend time. Therefore, try to be with wise people and surround yourself with good advisors. Remember that *two can accomplish more than twice as much as one, for the results can be much better. If one falls, the other pulls him up; but if a man falls when he is alone, he is in trouble. Also, on a cold night, two under the same blanket gain warmth from each other but how can one be warm alone? And one standing alone can be attacked and defeated, but two can stand back-to-back and conquer; three is even better, for a triple-braided cord is not easily broken.*

"*Joy fills hearts that are planning for good!* Passion comes from the heart. It is the fire within! The key to creating passion in our lives is to realize our unique talents and our special role and purpose in the world. One good question to ask ourselves is: What one great thing would I dare to dream if I knew I was absolutely guaranteed success? If we imagine that we had the money, the time, the education, the contacts, the resources, and everything else that we could possibly need to achieve any one big goal, what would our goal in life then be?

"*Give me neither poverty nor riches! Give me just enough to satisfy my needs.* To dream of the future we desire does not mean that all things are good for us, that we should seek all we desire. To be content with what we have and understand what is most important for us helps us move in the right direction in our lives. When we set our goals we should consider how to

> "*Give me neither poverty nor riches! Give me just enough to satisfy my needs.*"

be of value and service to others. To work for greater purposes than our own desires is the key to being truly blessed.

"Hard work brings prosperity; playing around brings poverty. The future is not obscure or magical; when we eventually get there, the future is just like today. We build our future one day at a time until we are there. The present is the only thing we have. It is what we make of each day that makes a difference, taking one step at a time and working toward our dreams and goals. Only action can transform dreams into reality. *Do you know a hard-working man? He shall be successful and stand before kings!*

"If you don't plow in the cold, you won't eat at the harvest. Discipline is doing what we have to do and paying the price to bring the vision into reality. To give up something good now for something that is even better in the future. Everything has its price. If we want more, we need to give more. If we want to have a higher yield, we need to plough and sow more. The natural law on the development and growth always applies. We reap what we sow. If we want our dreams to come true, we prepare ourselves and pay the price in the training, performance, time, and effort it takes. One small step, and one sacrifice, after another.

"Be patient and you will finally win."

"Be patient and you will finally win. Most things worth striving for take time to achieve. This is true for financial success as well as skill in a certain area. It also takes consistency and persistence to become wise and build inner harmony and insight. Consistency is a matter of staying on

track. *Hope deferred makes the heart sick; but when dreams come true at last, there is life and joy.*

"*Steady plodding brings prosperity; hasty speculation brings poverty.* Perseverance is the true measure of the belief in ourselves and our ability to succeed. We all experience moments when everything seems dark and hopeless, but if we only persevere we will overcome every setback. The dark will give way and hope will return when dawn is transformed to daylight. We are sometimes tempted to take shortcuts to reach our goals sooner. Hasty speculation may seem like a good idea, but sooner or later impatience leads to a poor heart and an empty pocketbook. Only by performing work that creates bigger value will we achieve true success, financially as well as emotionally.

"*Look straight ahead; don't even turn your head to look.* Diversions of all kind are all around us. We have to work patiently and persistently fixing our eyes on our goal. We picture success and imagine our dream coming true. We hear the cheers and compliments of people we respect. In our mind we are enjoying the fruits of

> *"Look straight ahead; don't even turn your head to look."*

our work. Using our imagination this way, feeling the pride of accomplishment, our confidence and hope will increase. So we keep our eyes on our goals and they will remain close to our hearts, giving us the passion and the power to achieve each and every day. Once we can see it, we can be it.

"*Whatever you do, do well.* When we are putting passion, love, and gratitude into whatever we are doing, delivering more than what's expected, our achievements will shine like the rising sun. We earn the reputation of someone who produces great value. By setting our own standards and living accordingly, we become satisfied with ourselves and our worth will increase a thousandfold.

"*The wise man saves for the future, but the foolish man spends whatever he gets.* Those who work purposefully will eventually have the opportunity to achieve financial success. In order to do this we need to save part of our income for the future. Saving might seem almost magical to some who cannot fathom the long-term growth. After one day, one week, or one month, the difference appears nonexistent; but the benefits will be very obvious within a few years.

"*It is possible to give away and become richer! It is also possible to hold on too tightly and lose everything. Yes, the liberal man shall be rich! By watering others, he waters himself.* Giving is the key to prosperity and joyful living. When we value an abundance mentality, we see life as a source of ever enlarging opportunities, resources, and wealth. We are genuinely happy for other people's success. Sharing oneself and one's blessings with others brings happiness and satisfaction.

"*Give generously for your gifts will return to you later.* This is one of the most wonderful lessons in life. It is by giving to others that we ourselves receive. When we give a lot, we get a lot back. Our happiness lies in giving, not in getting. There are so many ways to give and serve that we will never run out of opportunities to help others. By concentrating on the good and radiating positive feelings, we spread happiness and energy around us. As we seek out the good in every situation, in what we see and experience, our lives will be filled with gratitude; we release our inner strength and energy. It's the law of the harvest that governs; we will always reap what we sow."

"Give generously for your gifts will return to you later."

The Queen of Sheba took in Solomon's every word. Then she asked permission to retire and time to reflect on his wisdom. Solomon bid her farewell, asking her to return the following morning by the palace gates, as he had a surprise for her.

She crossed the broad marble floor and exited to the back gardens. The afternoon sun was bright and the heat struck her as she stepped outside. To her left was a cobblestone walking path behind which the royal water reservoirs could be seen. Between the path and the reservoirs, trees and bushes stretched all the way to the door, creating an illusion of standing at the edge of a forest with the sun streaming through the greenery.

The Queen of Sheba continued ambling through the gardens, sweet fragrances filling her senses. Sitting down in the grass by a cedar tree, she began to think about her future and what she wanted to accomplish. She leaned her head back into the shade cast by the crown of an immense tree. She sat like this for a long time before she made the following decision:

"From now on I will clarify my vision and refine the path to my future. I will form internal pictures, like a picture of Solomon's palace, creating the life that I want to live and the person and leader I want to become during my journey. I will make a plan so my accomplishments become steps in the direction of the dream I keep closest to my heart!

"From now on I will work more purposefully. I will outline a daily routine to keep me on track, always doing my best, one day at a time, one step at a time. I will work toward my future with passion, setting my own standards for how hard I want to push myself. When things do not go exactly the way I planned, I will seek out competent people for support. My plans will be successful because I will choose good advisors.

"From now on I will work patiently and persistently keeping my eyes on my goal far ahead of me, because this helps me to better handle various situations along the way. The vision of what I want to accomplish and contribute to becomes my source of energy. As the plan gradually takes shape, I gain confidence and strength to persevere. I will also remember to enjoy what I accomplish during my journey. Whatever happens, the most important thing is that I grow and develop as a person through my efforts. This gives me life experience and satisfaction and will greatly enrich my life."

———————

My Own Reflections

Clarify the Vision for Your Desired Future!

"Anxious hearts are very heavy but a word of encouragement does wonders!"

—King Solomon

5

Create and Nurture Good Relationships

The twirling cloud of sand from the dry ground had just settled and the sun perched high in the sky, at the moment burning a little less intensely than usual. The royal wagon stood ready by the palace doors. It was a sight to be seen, built of wood from Lebanon's forests, with poles crafted of fine silver and a backrest of gold. On the crimson-colored seat was inscribed: *A token of our love, from the maidens of Jerusalem*.

The wagon emanated a scent of myrrh, incense, and spices. Two beautiful white Arabian horses were hitched to the shafts. The reins and bridle were made of good, strong leather and the bits in the horses' mouths were pure gold. The animals stepped impatiently back and forth and tossed their flowing manes and plumage. The wagon was surrounded by a guard of sixty war-hardened soldiers with swords sheathed but ready to defend the king.

The Queen of Sheba was escorted to the wagon, and servants lifted her into the comfortable seat. Today she and Solomon would visit several cities that Solomon had built; they were vital merchant centers with great storehouses for grain and goods. One city accommodated Solomon's horses and wagons. Another, the port city of Elot in Edom, was home to Solomon's navy, which was a gift from King Hiram. The ships with Hiram's experienced crew and Solomon's men transported gold, algumwood, and precious stones from Ofir. Algumwood was used in the construction of staircases in the Temple and the palace, as well as the psaltery for the Temple choir, and for harps and other musical instruments.

They traveled through villages crammed with tiny houses and yards. The Queen of Sheba saw goats and sometimes oxen and cows grazing in the hillsides. Further down the road they met caravans with camels and donkeys loaded with balm, honey, spices, myrrh, pistachio nuts, almonds, and dates heading for the markets in Jerusalem. After visiting some of Solomon's construction projects, they continued onward to the port city of Elot.

When they reached Elot, a cool breeze off the ocean wafted above them bringing the salty smells of the sea. The ships lay waiting in the harbor with their shiny foredecks made of cypress trees from the southern coast of Cyprus, with their oak oars bobbing up and down in the waves. After an initial inspection of the ships and their crews, Solomon suddenly asked the Queen, "Would you like to sail on one of these ships?"

The queen said yes without hesitation and their mood was cheerful as they boarded one of the fine vessels.

The wind was fair when they weighed anchor, and the sails, made of the finest linen in Egypt, billowed to drive the boat out into the harbor. The sound of the waves hitting the stern of the ship was punctuated with the captain's commands barked from the helm. Solomon pointed to some fishermen who had just placed their nets in the water and said, "Tonight we will enjoy fresh fish for dinner." Then he leaned against the railing and, looking out over the sea, said, "Let me continue to answer your question about the right principles for a successful life."

"If we want true success in life, we
need to create and nurture good relationships."

"No man is an island. In order to succeed in something, almost no matter what it is, we need help and support from others. Good relationships open the doors to all kinds of possibilities. We grow and develop in such relationships, making our lives more fulfilling. It is also the base for our leadership.

"A man will always reap just the kind of crop he sows. When we do good to others they will also do good to us. We will always reap what we sow. The basic principle for good relationships is well known: Treat others the way you want to

"A man will always reap just the kind of crop he sows."

> When we do good to others they will also do good to us. We will always reap what we sow.

be treated, with the same respect regardless of position in society. For each person is unique and valuable and is a part of creation. We respect the opinions of others, their competence, time, and differences because this is how we want to be treated by others. When we live according to this principle, we will enrich the lives of many people, and because we reap what we sow, our own lives will also be enriched and flourish.

"Pride ends in destruction; humility ends in honor. While we need to sense the importance of what we are doing, we need to see it with a sense of smallness of our own part. A person who builds good relationships is humble and friendly in his interactions with others. That individual knows that pride and self-righteousness are unfortunate characteristics. For even if we are successful and have reached a high position in society, we need to consider the following: Are we really as important as we think we are? Would the world come to an end if we were not here? What have we gained from wealth and pomp? Everything disappears like the shadow of a messenger hurrying by; a ship sailing the high seas does not leave a trace, its keel does not carve a trench through the water. Nor does a bird flying through the sky leave any trail of its flight. The power of its wing-strokes cuts a path through

the light air, but the path is invisible to the eye. Or, like an arrow moving toward its target, the air parts as the arrow slips through it, and no one can see the arrow's path.

"In this perspective, we should be aware of our own insignificance in the scheme of things, and we should approach others with a sense of humility as we move along. A truly successful person does not feel the need to call attention to himself or his achievements. Nor does he regard himself as better than others. He knows who he is and is secure within himself.

"*Anxious hearts are very heavy but a word of encouragement does wonders!* Everybody needs encouragement and attention. By encouraging another person with a kind word, a helpful suggestion, or an expression of admiration, we show our belief in that person, and we plant the seeds of hope. Where a seed of hope has been planted, self-confidence and belief in the future will grow and reap progress and enjoyment.

> *"Anxious hearts are very heavy but a word of encouragement does wonders!"*

"We can begin our day by recognizing people we meet with a kind word or a smile. A smile is like the rays of the sun—it spreads warmth and encouragement. Like a flower withers away and dies without water, a person also withers away inside without encouragement and attention.

"*Gentle words cause life and health; griping brings discouragement.* Words hold a miraculous power. Yes, words possess their own magic. They can evoke feelings of happiness or sadness, enthusiasm or hopelessness. Words can harm or hurt just like the sharpest sword or arrow. Words can also heal, bringing health and strength to the receiver. The words we say to others and what we tell ourselves are critical. I cannot emphasize this enough. We have to think about what we say and choose our words carefully because our words can either bring pain and suffering, or create vitality, health, and energy for others and ourselves. *Kind words are like honey—enjoyable and healthful.*

> *"In the end, people appreciate frankness more than they do flattery."*

"In the end, people appreciate frankness more than they do flattery. Our interest in others must be honest and genuine, an approach that fills us with thoughtfulness and respect. However, if we are only interested in others as a means to get what we want for ourselves, any success we might have will not last. People will see through our motives and lose their trust in us. And trust is the basis for good relations and lasting success.

"Pleasant sights and good reports give happiness and health. As we seek out the good in what we see and experience, we release our inner strength and energy. There is always something positive to convey. By concentrating on the good and radiating positive feelings, happiness and energy blossoms around us.

"Everyone enjoys giving good advice, and how wonderful it is to be able to say the right thing at the right time! There is a right time and a wrong time to share your thoughts with others. Negative comments should be discussed in privacy while positive feedback may be shared in public as it brings recognition and satisfaction. We should carefully consider where and when we are most likely to get a good response.

"From a wise mind comes careful and persuasive speech. When we argue in favor of our beliefs and opinions, we should be aware that certain words create resistance. The wise man chooses his words carefully and considers the effect they may have. He avoids statements and directives that may provoke resistance and disputes. Instead, he asks questions or presents his case in the form of suggestions, initiating a dialogue. *A good man thinks before he speaks.*

> *"From a wise mind comes careful and persuasive speech."*

"Be patient and you will finally win, for a soft tongue can break hard bones. If we proceed too quickly and too eagerly when we want the cooperation or support of others, we are likely to meet resistance. On the other hand, if we are patient, calm, and flexible, people will take interest in our ideas.

"If you profit from constructive criticism you will be elected to the wise men's hall of fame. But to reject criticism is to harm yourself and your own best interests. If we want to maintain good relations we must learn to handle criticism, to listen,

learn, and be flexible enough to change. Constructive criticism from others helps us to grow and correct our behavior. And remember: There is always something to learn!

"Don't refuse to accept criticism; get all the help you can.

"Don't refuse to accept criticism; get all the help you can. We all need other people's views reflecting how we are doing. Being open to criticism along the way will help us succeed. If we experience unfair criticism, remember that those who want to accomplish something often encounter resistance from others. Perhaps they are actually jealous of our successes. What is important is how we react to criticism. Generally, the best way to handle petty or unfair criticism is not to react at all. If we do not let ourselves be provoked, the criticism will eventually disappear by itself. On the other hand, if the criticism concerns important issues or our deepest values, we must respond with all the power, wisdom, and intelligence we possess. A person who is honest and true has nothing to fear.

"The wise man learns by listening. A wise man knows the importance of being a good listener. First he tries to understand, then to be understood. He never joins in a conversation without knowing what it is about, the full context. Few people really listen, and still it is an investment with excellent returns. Besides learning from listening, we also create opportunities for good relations. By being a good

listener we show our interest in others, demonstrating that we care about them.

"A wise man listens to others. Really listening requires our full attention. It is impossible to listen half-heartedly. Listening requires an ability to feel and empathize, which creates understanding as well

"A wise man listens to others."

as deeper and stronger relationships. Being non-judgmental in discussions and attempting to understand the standpoint of others is to show love."

Suddenly a high wave rushed over the railing of the ship and a cascade of water splashed the Queen of Sheba and King Solomon. They quickly stepped back from the railing, their hair and clothes drenched. Wiping their eyes, they looked at each other, first in surprise and then they broke out in laughter. One of the crewmembers hurriedly offered them linen cloths to dry themselves off, and inquired whether they were unharmed. Solomon smiled and answered, "We are fine. The sea just wanted to make us more attentive to its power and surprised us with a shower." Then he turned to the Queen of Sheba and asked if she was okay. She smiled and nodded her head while a drop of water lingered and sparkled in her hair before it slowly fell onto the wet linen.

"Well, this was a refreshing break, but now I will try to collect myself and share a few more thoughts on how to build good relations," he said as he draped the dry cloth around his shoulders, absorbing lingering dampness.

"Once when I was riding my horse in the mountains, I came upon a peculiar sight. A large mountain goat made its way along a winding path on the mountainside. It was an impressive ram with enormous corkscrew-shaped horns. The path was narrow and the drop-off from the edge stretched all the way to the bottom of the valley. Suddenly another mountain goat appeared on the same path but from the other side of the mountain; another ram with similar big, backward-bent horns. They each walked slowly along the path and suddenly caught sight of each other.

"I held my horse and hardly dared breathe in anticipation of what I might witness next. I knew mountain goats are skilled climbers, but in this particular place the only way to proceed was along the narrow path. They were about to meet and would not be able to pass each other without a certain life-or-death fight. In my younger days, I had witnessed mountain goats fight and had been amazed at the power with which they attacked. And there they were on the cliff ledge, two powerful mountain goats, staring each other down. Turning around was impossible. I could tell they were preparing to fight as their hoofs scraped the rocks.

"They were about to charge at each other when I witnessed something very strange. One of the mountain goats fell down on its front knees. It lay on the path as if dead, letting the other animal step on its body and pass over it. It was all over before I had time to blink and I could barely believe my eyes. The goat struggled to its feet, shook itself a bit, and the two goats continued on the narrow path along the cliff wall.

"This wonder of nature made me realize that if we humble ourselves and avoid unnecessary conflict, both parties win and may continue forward. But it requires inner strength to humble oneself and remain calm. *A wise man stays cool when insulted. This is his strength.*

"*A soft answer turns away wrath, but harsh words cause quarrels.* Conflicts between people are inevitable. Sooner or later, conflicts will occur in all relationships. Experiencing different views is a healthy thing. Nobody possesses the whole truth. If we use our listening skills, ask questions, and try to understand

> *"A soft answer turns away wrath, but harsh words cause quarrels."*

others' opinions and reasoning, we are closer to a solution. A soft answer makes it easier to settle a dispute.

"*Do not repay evil for evil. Wait for the Lord to handle the matter.* When someone is hurtful or treats us unfairly, we shall not return this treatment or become vengeful. We reap what we sow. Sooner or later, unjust practices will catch up with a wrongdoer. *The man who sets a trap for others will get caught in it himself.* But if we leave what happened behind us, we can go on with inner peace. *If your enemy is hungry, give him food! If he is thirsty, give him something to drink! This will make him feel ashamed of himself, and God will reward you.*

"*An angry man is silenced by giving him a gift!* If it is possible for us to promote friendship, then we should do everything we can to achieve this. Presenting someone with a gift can transform hostility to friendship.

"Love forgets mistakes; nagging about them parts the best of friends. A wise man does not carry a grudge or dwell on injustices. He considers a mistake as a springboard to insight. Therefore he also acknowledges mistakes, both his own and others', and is quick to forgive. A forgiving attitude toward oneself and others brings inner peace and harmony.

> *"Truth stands the test of time; lies are soon exposed."*

"Truth stands the test of time; lies are soon exposed. To be successful in relationships, we need to be totally honest and truthful. However, honesty is not the same as completely speaking our minds in every situation. In consideration of others, a wise person does not always reveal what he believes immediately. But at the same time, he is fully aware that evasive words and white lies will soon be discovered. When telling the truth, we need not worry about being caught in a lie or forgetting what we said. Therefore we can confidently move forward. Honesty and truthfulness are the foundation for good relationships.

"If you must choose, take a good name rather than great riches; for to be held in loving esteem is better than silver and gold. Our reputation is a shield that we must protect with great care. Dishonesty, unjust gain, and self-interest

quickly destroy our good reputation and credibility. Nothing lasting can be formed without credibility. A reputation of trustworthiness is more valuable than precious stones. A good reputation brings us many opportunities, as well as happiness, self-esteem, and satisfaction.

"Gossip separates the best of friends. If you feel like you have to spread a rumor, flee from this thought by walking down to the sea and writing your words in the sand so they will be swept away forever by the tide. Gossip and rumors are destructive to others and are also destructive to ourselves. When we do not have anything good to say about somebody, it is better not to say anything at all. We will be more content in the long run.

"Do not praise yourself; let others do it! If we want to succeed in relationships, we should avoid commending and calling attention to ourselves. Instead, by praising others and giving them credit, they will thrive and some of the honor will be bestowed upon us, too. In the end, we will also receive recognition.

"Your own soul is nourished when you are kind; it is destroyed when you are cruel. When we show kindness toward others, they will seek our company. In addition to making many friends, we will also enjoy an inner peace. We will shape a healthy soul within

> *"Your own soul is nourished when you are kind; it is destroyed when you are cruel."*

ourselves. Everything we do toward others, we in turn do to ourselves. If we are cruel to others, the wellspring of life within us becomes contaminated, and we feel ill. But if we are kind to others, the inner source of our well-being is renewed.

"Most people will tell you what loyal friends they are, but are they telling the truth?" True concern is shown with actions; being available when someone needs us, or offering counsel when someone is headed in the wrong direction. A person who is sincere, truthful, and fair will be highly respected and his ties of friendship will be stronger. We should treasure friends who are loyal and whom we fully trust, because there are few we will encounter in life. *Open rebuke is better than hidden love! Wounds from a friend are better than kisses from an enemy!*

> *"The man who tries to be good, loving and kind finds life, righteousness and honor."*

"The man who tries to be good, loving and kind finds life, righteousness and honor. By treating others lovingly and kindly we build good, long-lasting relationships. We accept and love people just the way they are. We look to their strengths instead of their weaknesses, their assets instead of their shortcomings.

"When we discover something good in a person and share our discovery with this person, we also help in that individual's development as a person. Our reward for this is much more valuable than money or possessions. People will grow and prosper around us and we will achieve satisfaction and peace of mind."

The sun was setting into the horizon and the wind decreased into a pleasant breeze as the Queen of Sheba and King Solomon sailed into Elot harbor. The queen had enjoyed the time at sea, and treasured the words of wisdom Solomon had shared with her.

They arrived by the dock and stepped ashore as the sun disappeared into the sea. The Queen of Sheba could still feel the ground move under her feet, as if the waves had followed her onto dry ground. Not much was said on the way home, as both felt tired from the day's adventures.

The closeness and warmth of King Solomon and the steady sound of the horses' hooves against the ground filled the Queen of Sheba with a comfortable, drowsy relaxation. She rested her head against Solomon's shoulder and dreamed about how to make use of Solomon's words and put them into action:

———————————

"From now on I will create and nurture good relationships. I will value people and relationships more than gold and treat those I encounter, stranger as well as a close friend, the way I would like them to treat me. With the respect and dignity we all deserve. I will accept them as they are, for each person is a unique, valuable part of creation.

"From now on I will speak well of others or else remain quiet. My tongue is a double-edged sword that can form words to improve or destroy relationships. I will establish trust by being honest, straightforward, and truthful. While I strive to be compassionate and sensitive, I will first try to understand, then to be understood! I will seek mutual understanding and always be open to other peoples view on how I am doing. When I fall short or make a mistake, which is human, I will show a humble spirit, acknowledge my mistake, and correct it. When others make mistakes I will have a forgiving attitude.

"From now on I will support people around me, providing honest and rightful appreciation and giving them encouraging words along the way. When I give advice and guidance, I will first carefully consider how to best express my thoughts to be constructive and choose the right moment. By showing respect and friendship I will maintain good relationships wherever I go and my heart will be filled with joy and happiness."

My Own Reflections

"Have two goals: wisdom—that is, knowing and doing what is right— and common sense. Do not let them slip away, for they fill you with living energy, and are a feather in your cap."

—King Solomon

6

Stay True to Your Own Governing Values

The desert storm struck Jerusalem, blanketing everything with sandy granules. The sun was barely visible through the clouds of sand. Servants and advisors on their way to Solomon's palace wrapped their mantles and scarves tightly around them in attempts to shield their faces from the abrasive wind. Still, it found its way under and through the material, giving them a mouthful of gritty dust.

The Queen of Sheba was once again on her way to see King Solomon, after her usual private time in the morning. But the windblown debris seemed to bring trouble along with it, and Solomon was forced to reschedule their meeting when his schedule became packed with obligations. However, just as the queen was about to make her way back to the guest quarters, Solomon invited her to sit with his advisors and elders, who were perched in the balcony to the right of the throne.

One of the many disputes King Solomon had to settle this morning concerned three men who came before him. One of them stated:

"We were traveling when the Sabbath fell. We told each other, 'Come, let us hide our money somewhere safe while we rest,' which we did. After the Sabbath, when we were getting ready to set out again, we found that our money was gone.

"I am innocent, Your Majesty, but one of the others here must have taken the money because no one else knew the hiding place." The other two men defended themselves, proclaiming their innocence and implicating one of the others.

King Solomon listened quietly to the three men. Then he commented, "I have been informed that you are businessmen with a good education. Is this correct?" The men agreed that this was true, and Solomon continued, "Then you are also well-versed in legal matters and I want to hear your opinion about the following:

"A king from a Nordic country has asked my advice regarding an incident in his kingdom. It concerns a young man and woman who lived on the same farm and fell in love with each other. They met when they were very young and saw each other frequently, but when their parents wanted them to marry, they were still not ready. Instead, they promised their parents that neither one would ask for someone else's hand without the other's approval. And they took an oath on it.

"A while later, the girl fell in love with another man. When he arrived to ask for her hand in marriage and to take her with him, she said, 'I cannot become your wife until my friend has given his approval.'

"Hearing this, the suitor suggested, 'Let us go to your friend and ask him to set you free of your promise.' So they went to him and said, 'Please take all the silver and gold you want and set me free from my promise.' And the friend replied, 'You have kept your word and I will not stand in the way of your happiness. I free you from your promise and I decline what is rightly mine.' Then he addressed the young man and told him, 'Keep your silver and gold and rejoice in each other.' And the happy couple went on their way.

"On their way home they were attacked by robbers. One of the robbers, an old man, captured the girl and took all the silver and gold they carried, even the jewelry she wore. But when he tried to assault her, the girl pleaded with him, 'I beg you, wait until I have told you my story!'

"She told the old man everything that had happened, and added, 'If the man who loved me could restrain his desire for me despite his youthful vigor, and would not use me when we were young and in love—and furthermore he did not take my gold now when I offered it to him—you who are old and worthy of respect, and who ought to fear God every moment, should restrain your passion and let me walk away untouched. Take all the silver, gold, and jewels I have, but let me go in peace with my betrothed.'

"When the robber heard this, he lifted his eyes toward the blue sky and thought to himself, 'Should an old man who is soon going to die do something like that?'"

Solomon asked the three men, "What did he do?" Before they had time to answer, he continued, "The old robber let her go with her betrothed and also returned all the silver, gold, and jewels he had stolen from her.

"And now the king of the Nordic country has asked me to determine who deserves the most respect. Tell me now, who do you think is most admirable in this story?"

The first of the merchants said, "I admire the girl who remembered her oath and kept her promise. She is most admirable." The second one said, "I admire the young man who restrained himself in his youth and now set the girl free from her promise without taking the gold. I think this is most admirable." The third man said, "I admire the robber who had taken the silver and gold and then returned it and did not assault the girl." Then he added hesitantly and with a fleeting look of greed in his eyes, "For even if he let the girl go, he could have kept the money."

Solomon concluded, pointing to the third man, "If this man yearns for money he has not even seen after hearing this story, how much more would he yearn for money he has seen?" As Solomon ordered the man arrested, the man fell to his knees and confessed. He promised to disclose where the money was hidden and asked for mercy. As the thief was taken away, Solomon declared to all who were gathered

"Dishonest gain will never last, so why take the risk?"

in the throne hall, *"Dishonest gain will never last, so why take the risk?"*

After the verdict, it was time for a break before the other cases were heard. Solomon turned to the queen who had listened to the three men. "Come, and let us take a walk. There is something I want to show you. I think you will find it very interesting."

They left the throne hall through the side door to the garden, where the air was now cool and refreshing. The wind had died down, leaving small sand piles on the garden path. Now the sun's rays found their way through the trees, casting shadows on the stonewall in front of them.

They walked along the path and after a short time arrived at the Temple. The main part of the Temple was paneled with cypress wood, plated with pure gold, and engraved with palm trees and chains. A large ornamental portal with two copper pillars on each side adorned the opening. The pillars were amply decorated and each had a name. The pillar to the south was called Jakin, which means, "God is our support." The other pillar was called Boas, which means, "God is our strength." An annex was located on both sides along the entire length of the Temple, facing the outer stonewalls. Each of the three floors had one row of narrow windows.

King Solomon and the Queen of Sheba stopped in front of the entrance to the Temple. Solomon proudly told her how it took him seven and a half years to build the Temple that he had promised his father, King David. The project had involved seventy thousand people just to carry the stones to Jerusalem from the quarries where they had been cut into blocks.

They passed through the portal and entered the hall, which smelled of incense. Solomon pointed out the cedar panels with ornate carvings in the shape of rosebuds and other flowers covering the interior from floor to ceiling. The queen also admired the floorboards of grained cypress wood.

Within the Temple, at one end, was the most sacred room—the Holy of Holies. This room measured nine meters in length and nine meters in width and was nine meters high. This too was overlaid with finest gold. Twenty-six-ounce gold nails were used. Two sculptured statues of angels, carved from olive wood, stood on the floor facing the outer room. They were placed so that their outspread wings stretched wingtip to wingtip across the room, from wall to wall. Across the entrance to this room he had placed a veil of blue and crimson finely spun linen, decorated with angels. Gold chains protected the entrance. King Solomon explained that he could not show the Queen of Sheba this room because only the high priest was allowed to enter.

After completing the tour of the Temple, they sat down in one of the side-rooms. The queen told Solomon he was correct when he expected the tour to be of interest to her. "It was both interesting and exciting to hear the Temple's history. But tell me, why are we not allowed to enter the inner room?"

King Solomon answered, "The inner room is holy and only the high priest may enter. This is where the Ark of the Covenant, containing the two stone tablets with the commandments, is kept. The tablets were given to our forefather Moses by the Lord on the mountain of Sinai."

"Why do you have these commandments and what do they mean?" asked the queen.

Solomon answered, "The ten commandments are the guiding principles of our people. They contain instructions for how we should live our lives. According to the commandments, we shall direct our energy toward God where everything originates and ends; we shall protect and preserve life in all forms; we shall respect the properties and rights of others; we shall be dependable in thought, words, and actions. All the commandments may be summed up in the single statement that we shall love our neighbors as we love ourselves. When we respect these rules and live according to them, we also lay the foundation for a successful life and functioning society.

"Let me tell you about two men I heard about who went for a walk in the beautiful Basan mountains. This happened in the winter where the impressive snow-covered mountains stretched as far as they could see. Several small villages were located in the mountains, inhabited mainly by hermits supporting themselves by growing fruit, wine, and olives. The men were on their way to one of these villages. It was a long journey and they spent their time talking when they suddenly were surprised by bad weather. The wind increased and turned colder, blowing snow all around them. They still had a long way to walk to the next village where they could take cover.

"Suddenly they heard a weak call for help. After trekking a little further, they found a man who had fallen in the snow and broken his leg. He was weak and cold and pleaded with the two men for help. 'We must help him!' cried one of the men through the howling wind. 'We can't just leave him here to die.' The man removed his mantle and covered the injured man. But his companion cried over the bitter wind, 'We have to leave him or we will all die! It is too far to walk and the road is too steep. We have to think of ourselves!'

"'No,' objected the first man. 'We have to do what we can to save him,' and he bent down and tucked the mantle closer around the injured man. Then he carefully lifted him onto his back and began staggering ahead in the snow.

"The second man shouted, 'You are crazy. I will walk ahead and leave you if you don't want to save your own life. It's up to you.' He left and soon disappeared in the falling snow.

"The man with the injured person on his back proceeded along the road but had to stop and rest frequently. Several hours went by and he became very tired and sweaty from the exertion. Just as he thought they might die in the snow, he noticed a light ahead of him. 'A house!' he cried, 'we are going to make it!' Then he suddenly stumbled over something. To his horror, he discovered his travel companion laying frozen to death in the snow.

"He pushed forward and finally arrived at the house where he and the injured man were invited into the warmth. When the man told his story, one of the people in the house said. 'Your unselfishness saved you. You risked your life to help someone in need. The effort of carrying the heavy load and the warmth you provided each other helped you to survive.'"

Solomon continued, "Only he who thinks of the welfare of others and not only of himself and his possessions can live a successful life. He who loves his fellow men and unselfishly helps those in need will succeed. Our behavior toward other people is linked with our values."

> "If we want true success in life, we need to stay true to our own governing values."

"Our values determine our actions. They help us determine what is important to us in life and what we want to stand for. Being aware of our values makes it easier for us to make the right decisions in life. We are better able to choose our priorities so our steps always take the right direction.

"Have two goals: wisdom— that is, knowing and doing what is right—and common sense. Do not let them slip away, for they fill you with living energy, and are a feather in your cap. Wisdom is not the same as knowledge, experience, or intelligence. Rather, wisdom is how we use those

> *"Have two goals: wisdom—that is, knowing and doing what is right—and common sense."*

> Wisdom is not the same as knowledge, experience, or intelligence. Rather, wisdom is how we use those qualities in an ethical and morally sound way.

qualities in an ethical and morally sound way. It's a deep insight of what is true, right, and lasting, something that every human being has to value during a lifetime.

"The man who wants to do right will get a rich reward. But the man who wants to get rich quick will quickly fail. All of us run into conflicts regarding our desires, what we want to do, and what we ought to do. Living according to our values, the things we know are true and right, frees us from inner conflicts that consume our energy and vitality. This is when we may call ourselves whole persons. Our lips will not contradict the feelings of our heart. Living according to our values means that we will experience confidence and inspiration in what we do.

"A man's conscience is the Lord's searchlight exposing his hidden motives. Our conscience reveals to us when we act against our inner convictions. But the voice of the conscience is so soft that hearing it takes sensitivity and perceptiveness. When we follow our inner convictions, we have a clean conscience and can rest without fear. We can look ourselves in the mirror before we go to bed and feel proud of ourselves. And remember: There is no softer pillow than a clean conscience.

"I would have you learn this great fact: that a life of doing right is the wisest life there is. If you live that kind of life, you will not limp or stumble as you run. Carry out my instructions; do not forget them, for they will lead you to real living. It takes self-discipline and character to do the right thing and uphold the truth. By human nature, we search for the fastest and easiest way to reach our goals instead of considering the long-term consequences of our actions.

"Before every man there lies a wide and pleasant road that seems right but ends in death. Taking the wide road is easier than taking the narrow road. The narrow-road approach requires far more effort and does not provide immediate rewards.

"The man who knows right from wrong, and has good judgment and common sense is happier than the man who is immensely rich! We are sometimes faced with difficult decisions. Perhaps we receive certain advantages or financial profit by making choices that aren't necessarily righteous. But we need to stop and think. What happens to our self-respect if we act against our governing values? We lose energy and vitality. When we are tempted to do what we suspect is wrong, we need to ask ourselves three questions.

> *"The man who knows right from wrong, and has good judgment and common sense is happier than the man who is immensely rich!"*

"First ask 'Is this permissible and fair?' If it is not fair to the involved parties but creates an imbalance in your favor, do not proceed. You will reap what you sow.

"If the answer is 'yes,' then ask yourself a second question: How will I feel about myself if I do it? Will I be proud of myself and sleep well at night?' If you are unable to answer 'yes' to this question, do not proceed.

"The third and final question is: 'Can I tell my family and my friends about it? If I am not happy about telling my family and my friends about my decision, do not push forward to do it. The wide road you see ahead of you will lead you to trouble, because there is no right way to do the wrong thing.

> *"A little, gained honestly, is better than great wealth gotten by dishonest means."*

"*A little, gained honestly, is better than great wealth gotten by dishonest means.* The joy of achieving something we have longed for will only last if we achieved it in an honest manner. Possessing the self-discipline to do what is right builds our self-confidence. A fool takes the easy road but the wise man takes the right road.

"*A good man is guided by his honesty.* If we want to have true success in life, it is important to be honest and tell the truth in all situations. With honesty as a guiding light we are able to look in the mirror and say, 'I know I have done what is right.' This means having an image of yourself, knowing who you are and how you want to live. With honesty as a guiding light, one is always honest—not just when it suits us.

"It is better to have self-control than to control an army. When we live according to principles such as trustworthiness, respect, responsibility, honesty, integrity, loyalty, fairness, people's equal worth, and strive for development and improvement, we make progress

> *"It is better to have self-control than to control an army."*

and lay the foundation for a good life. It takes self-control and self-discipline to develop a character based on these principles. Self-discipline is doing what we have decided to do even when we do not feel like it. It is not what we say, but what we do that counts. If we practice what we preach, we enjoy credibility, inner happiness, and satisfaction. *If you want a long and satisfying life, closely follow my instructions. Never forget to be truthful and kind. Hold these virtues tightly. Write them deep within your heart."*

As Solomon talked, the sun hovered high in the sky, shining brightly on the Temple as Solomon and the Queen of Sheba walked to the outer forecourt. "I must return to my duties in the throne hall, but before we part I want to give you something to think about until we see each other again," Solomon said with certain sadness in his voice. Talking with the Queen of Sheba had become a stimulating part of his day, which was otherwise filled with obligations.

He turned toward the queen. "I want to ask you something that you may find strange but will help you see what is truly important in your life. Imagine that you attend the funeral of a dear friend. You and the other mourners are gathered around the deceased. You watch the sad faces of the family members and close friends. You hear their sobs mixed with the peaceful funeral music. One by one they approach the deceased to bid a last farewell. When it is your turn to step forward, you suddenly realize you are the dead person in the casket. You are attending your own funeral. The mourners have come to honor your memory. I ask you now to very carefully consider these questions: What do you want the mourners to say about you and the life you lived? What did you want to accomplish in life? What have you done for or meant to your family, friends, and acquaintances? What descriptions of yourself would make you the proudest? What are the weaknesses you hope no one discovered?

"If you sincerely consider this scenario, it will touch your deepest inner values. The answers to the questions will reveal the values that bring meaning to your life. You will begin to reflect over who you are, what you value the most, and what you wish to stand for. You are reminded that you should live your life knowing where you are going and what you want to leave behind."

They walked back to the throne hall in silence. As they reached the entrance of the hall, Solomon said, "I plan to arrange a farewell party in your honor the evening before you return to your country. Please prepare your entourage for this. If I have understood it correctly, your departure is scheduled for early next week."

The Queen of Sheba confirmed this and told Solomon she was eager to go home, but at the same time she would miss their conversations. Solomon took her hands in his and said, "I know I will miss them too." He let his eyes rest on hers for a moment before he turned and quickly disappeared into the throne hall.

The Queen of Sheba remained standing for a while in the hot garden before she returned to her rooms. She planned to keep to herself throughout the afternoon and reflect over what Solomon taught her this day.

Inside her suite, she padded over to the open windows facing the garden. She gazed dreamily out over the valley behind the garden wall, feeling a certain apprehension at the thought of leaving. To escape these feelings, which she did not understand, she sat down to think about Solomon's questions. These were important questions truly worth contemplating and answering. After a long while, she wrote on a piece of papyrus:

"From now on I will stay true to my governing values. I want to see my life in a bigger perspective with the goal of leaving something of lasting value behind. I will therefore make clear the values I want to stand for, and try to live accordingly. Only then can I move ahead with determination, full of energy.

"From now on I will base my values on time-tested principles. Only that which is founded on trustworthiness, respect, responsibility, honesty, integrity, loyalty, fairness, equality, and the desire for constant improvement will be of lasting value. These principles are like guiding lights in the dark; they lead me in the right direction.

"From now on I will choose the narrow road, make the difficult decisions, and do what I believe is right and fair. I will practice self-discipline and adhere to what I believe in and what I have decided to accomplish. I know I will be tried and tempted. At those times I will listen to my inner voice telling me which road is right for me. By living in harmony with my governing values and being true to myself, I will be able to live boldly and have inner peace maintaining the strength to be of service to other people."

———————

My Own Reflections

"*But all who listen to me (wisdom) shall live in peace and safety, unafraid.*"

—King Solomon

7

Go Beyond Guilt, Fear, and Worry

The day before the Queen of Sheba planned to return to her homeland, she was awakened by the sunshine coming through the vaulted windows that opened up to the garden. She slowly followed the rays with her eyes, then closed them and enjoyed the warmth and the sound of birds singing outside.

Suddenly she heard the faint sound of footsteps outside her door and was at once wide awake. Who would come to her door at this hour? She called on her attendant who immediately came to her bedside. "Did you too hear the sound outside my door?" she asked. They listened quietly, and hearing a knock on the door they looked at each other, puzzled. The queen pulled her nightgown tightly around her body, quickly slipped out of her bed, and disappeared into another room. Her attendant walked up to the door and asked in a loud voice what was going on. Outside the door the caller answered claiming that he had a message for the Queen of Sheba.

The attendant opened the door and one of King Solomon's most trusted men appeared. He presented a papyrus scroll tied with a red ribbon and marked with the royal seal. The attendant forwarded it to the queen, who broke the seal, rolled out the papyrus, and read: "Can you meet me in the garden as soon as you are done with your morning routine? I have something special to show you." The message was signed by Solomon.

After she dressed and ate her breakfast, she wondered why Solomon would send her a message in this manner. "Oh well. I will know soon enough," she thought as she left her suite to meet Solomon.

When she arrived at the path leading to the garden, she was met by one of Solomon's honorary guards. She was still wondering about the reason for the impromptu meeting as they proceeded along the path. As they approached the garden, she could see Solomon waiting for them. The guard greeted Solomon and then left them alone. Solomon welcomed her with a smile and said, "Come, let me show you something."

The Queen of Sheba's curiosity mounted as they walked together. After a moment, King Solomon pointed to a grove of trees. There, in the shadow by the stonewall, was a magnificent stallion with its reins tied around a cypress tree. The horse had a small head with large, widely placed eyes and a beautiful bowed neck. The mane was braided and appeared polished in the sunlight. Solomon approached the horse, then turned to the queen and said, "This is a farewell gift from me to you. You know that I am very interested in horses; therefore presenting you with one of my very finest stallions gives me great pleasure. This is a thoroughbred horse from Southern Arabia. His name is Manaki, meaning the horse with the beautiful neck."

The Queen of Sheba moved closer to the horse and attempted to pet his muzzle. But the horse pulled back, snorted loudly, and stomped his hooves. The queen withdrew her hand and said with a frightened smile, "I do not know if I dare accept a gift like this. He seems a bit too wild for my taste."

Solomon also smiled and answered, "Everything will be fine. He just needs to get to know you better. How about going for a ride?" Meanwhile, one of Solomon's servants had brought another beautiful stallion, Solomon's own horse. They mounted the horses, gently pressed their heels to the horses' girths, and began riding.

The Queen of Sheba and King Solomon rode at a steady pace and soon left Jerusalem behind them. Several kites sailed above them against the clear blue sky, gently flowing with the air current. They crossed a wide field and then began climbing upward through large groves of cedar trees. Fragrant pine needles crackled beneath the horses' hooves. In the distance, they could see gazelles and deer grazing in the meadow along the tree line. They rode for a while in silence, and then Solomon asked, "Well, how do you like my gift?" The Queen of Sheba replied that she had never ridden a better horse.

Leaving the forest behind them, a spectacular view opened up. The sight of a deep ravine with a silver-colored, winding river far below them took their breath away. While they enjoyed this view, a falcon soared above the water on broad wings, now and then diving into the river to catch its prey as water cascaded in every direction. It slowly ascended again, clutching the shiny fish in its claws. In the clear air they were able to follow the flight of the grand falcon for a long time until it disappeared in the shadows on the other side of the ravine.

Both the queen and king watched the display of nature in quiet awe from the horses' backs. Then Solomon straightened his back and said, "Is there anything more beautiful to watch than God's magnificent nature?"

The Queen of Sheba nodded in agreement and said, "This day promises to be a very special memory for me to take home." She had no idea how true this was.

Solomon nimbly dismounted his horse and offered the Queen of Sheba a helping hand. She did not take it, but got off her horse just as nimbly as Solomon did. Solomon's surprised expression caused her to laugh. Standing close to Solomon, she could feel a quivering sensation flow through her body.

They stood quietly for a moment before Solomon turned and removed a blanket and picnic basket from the saddlebags. He spread the blanket on the ground and produced a silver bowl containing juicy pheasant breasts, white bread, and a jug of wine. They sat down on the blanket and Solomon expressed his surprise and admiration of the queen's riding skills. "You have certainly withheld your experience with horses from me. Is there anything else I should know about?"

They both laughed and the queen replied, "One is entitled to keep a few secrets, I believe."

Solomon turned serious and said, "You have brought me great joy during your visit here. Only the farewell party tomorrow evening remains before you return home."

The Queen of Sheba did not answer immediately and her voice trembled when she replied, "Time flies in the presence of someone you hold dear."

Solomon appeared to want to say something but instead chose a pheasant breast from the silver bowl between them. He chewed in silence and then said, "Let me share a few more thoughts with you regarding the right principles for a successful life."

> "If we want true success in life, we need
> to go beyond guilt, fear, and worry."

"If we do not rid ourselves of these three demons they will drain us of energy and lust for life. Guilt and fear from events in our past follow us, leaving little room for love and happiness. Things we have done or said that we think was wrong. But what can we do about the past? Can we undo what has been done? Can we change the direction of the sand in the hourglass? No, it is not possible to change what has happened in the past, but it is possible to change our thoughts about what happened. Do not think of what happened as failures; instead look at them as experiences to learn from.

"A relaxed attitude lengthens a man's life; jealousy rots it away."

"*A relaxed attitude lengthens a man's life; jealousy rots it away.* A relaxed attitude comes from forgiving all those who have hurt us. Forgive and then forget. To forgive is to let go of what happened in a way that frees us from grudges and guilt. Life is too short to dwell on old mistakes. When we forgive others for what we think they have done to us, we are able to forgive ourselves as well. No one is perfect. No one is without blame. We all make mistakes and fall short. Consider how great it is that the Lord is willing to forgive those with a remorseful heart! We are freed from guilt and fear by living with the happiness and knowledge of being forgiven. So show the same generosity, and forgive others as well as yourself.

"*But all who listen to me shall live in peace and safety, unafraid.* Two emotions drive us: fear and trust. They do not mix any better than oil and water. Fear of failure, rejection, criticism, and inadequacy paralyzes and robs us of inner peace and confidence. When we listen to words of wisdom and always stay close to it, we will experience peace of mind, security, and trust.

"Jealousy is more dangerous and cruel than anger. The tendency to react with jealousy, discouragement, or anger depends on how we see ourselves and our surroundings. If we see ourselves not good enough to succeed, we consider the success of others unattainable to us and we react with envy. Oftentimes we believe our happiness or despair depends on luck or misfortune, something we are unable to control. By taking full responsibility for our freedom to choose how we react, we gain the power to grow regardless of external circumstances. We create these circumstances in our lives by looking inward for happiness, love, and peace.

"There is a legend that tells about an old man who had been very successful in business. He was immensely wealthy and had everything he needed, but there was one problem. He had a neighbor who was a businessman like himself and who had also been very successful, but the two did not get along. The old man felt his neighbor was more successful than he deserved to be. The old man was very envious, greedy, and

> By taking full responsibility for our freedom to choose how we react, we gain the power to grow regardless of external circumstances.

power-hungry, and he planned to accumulate even more power and profit to spite his neighbor. God saw this and decided to teach the man a lesson: that envy, jealousy, and greed for power is a dangerous combination, which leads to disaster.

"According to the legend, God sent the angel Gabriel to the man. Gabriel told the man he could wish for anything he wanted; there was no limit to what he could have or request. The angel also told the man that there was one thing he should know: God had decided that anything the man wished for and requested would also be given twofold to his neighbor.

"The man thought of all the things he wanted; more power, enormous wealth, perfect health, and an abundance of everything good in life. But then he pictured his neighbor and everything he would receive. He could not stand the thought of his neighbor receiving twice as much of everything and became enraged. The angel reminded him it was time to make a decision. The man thought a while longer and said, 'I have made up my mind. Make me blind in one eye.'

"This is what envy is; it destroys and tears apart. But envy does not hurt others as much as it hurts oneself. It may even make us sick and ruin our lives.

"The Lord is a strong fortress."

"*The Lord is a strong fortress.* The purpose of a fortress is to defend and protect against the enemy. The Lord is such a fortress against the enemy's arrows of guilt, fear, and worry. Love and forgiveness conquer these things. There is no fear in love.

Perfect love rejects the fear for the rest of our lives. The Lord is an impregnable fortress where we can find shelter, be safe, and gather courage.

"The wicked flee when no one is chasing them! But the godly are bold as lions! One cannot live life without courage. To have courage is to take charge of our lives and our fears. Powerful forces come to our aid when we act with courage. Just as the sun chases away the morning fog, our fear and worry disappear the moment we overcome what we fear or worry about.

"He who loves wisdom loves his own best interest and will be a success. The success we enjoy in life mainly depends on how we see ourselves. A positive self-image springs from loving wisdom and attracts success and happiness like the soil attracts the rain. Believing in ourselves is critical for success in life. Only when we love and appreciate ourselves can we live successful lives.

> *"He who loves wisdom loves his own best interest and will be a success."*

"In order to love others we need to love ourselves. We can only give away what we own. If we do not have money, we obviously cannot give away money. If we do not have love and harmony within ourselves, we cannot give it to others.

"Sever the roots of a tree and see how the leaves wither and the fruits fall off. To learn to love oneself, on the other hand, is like seeing the morning sun rise and dissolve the haze. The air turns clear and a new day begins. Suddenly everything is possible and little miracles take place all around you. Your health improves, your relationships become more satisfying, and you succeed in your efforts.

"To love yourself begins with accepting yourself the way you are—the good things as well as the faults and shortcomings. Even on a sunny day there are shadows. Good people also have dark sides. They do not deny them but strive forward, continually improving themselves.

"*Fear of man is a dangerous trap, but trust in God means safety.* Our level of self-esteem depends on what we think of ourselves and how we measure our accomplishments. Therefore, look at your possibilities. Do not compare yourself with others. Let the successes of others be an incentive for your own development. Believe in yourself. You are unique, an original created by the hand of a master. No one else is exactly like you.

> *"Get the facts at any price, and hold tightly to all the good sense you can get."*

"*Get the facts at any price, and hold tightly to all the good sense you can get.* It is your job to get to know and improve yourself. Devote some time to explore and find the truth in your own special distinctive character traits. A wise old man by the name of Susja was asked on his deathbed how he thought God's kingdom would be.

He answered, 'I do not know, but I know one thing. In my next life I will not be asked: Why were you not Moses? Why were you not David? Instead I will be asked: Why were you not Susja? Why were you not truly yourself?'

"Each of us has something precious that no one else has. Recognize what is precious within you. You are much better than you think. You possess great resources within you. You are like a seed that just has begun to grow. It will take some time, but with good soil and good care you will turn into a beautiful flower and provide fruit for many. In order to become a flower, we need to grow and develop, and growth always starts from the inside.

"To love oneself is also to love others regardless of their descent, background, race, or religion. The love you give is given back to you manifold. There are many kinds of people in the world; some build bridges, others build walls. Bridge-builders expect the best of other people. Wall-builders expect the worst and thereby create doubt and animosity. Love searches for the best within others.

"*There is a treasure in being good.* Only human beings have a need to be good. When we love and are loved, when we think and reflect, are generous and open, our lives become something more significant than just existing. The realization that we have a unique purpose in the world, to do good deeds, fills us with happiness and gratitude.

> *"There is a treasure in being good."*

"Our gratitude and joy grow as we realize how blessed we are already today. To be a part of this wonderful thing called 'life.' To have the opportunity to drink from wells that other people have dug. To warm ourselves from fires that other people have built. And sometimes to travel across bridges that other people have constructed. By the help of others, their guidance, their love, and their faith, our lives truly become meaningful and fulfilled.

"*The godly man's life is exciting.* A legend tells about a man who owned great tracts of land with fruit trees, plantations, and gardens. He was very wealthy and contented—contented because he was wealthy, and wealthy because he was contented.

"One day one of the wise men of the East paid him a visit. The wise man sat down by the fire and told about stones shaped into diamonds over the years in the depth of the ground. The diamonds were more valuable than anything else in the world and resembled gleaming drops of the sun. With diamonds like these, one could buy anything. A diamond the size of the man's thumb could buy huge parcels of land. With a whole mine full of diamonds one's children may take over the king's throne.

"After hearing about the huge value of diamonds, the man went to bed discontented—not because he had lost anything, but because he feared he was poor and he felt poor because he was discontented.

"He said to himself, 'I want those diamonds.' The following morning, when the sun rose above the rooftops, he went to the wise man and said, 'Could you tell me where I can find diamonds?' The wise man replied, 'Why do you need diamonds?' The man answered, 'I want to be extremely wealthy.' The wise man said, 'Well then, go look for them and you will find them.' But the man complained, 'I do not know where to look.' The old man said, 'Where you find a creek running like a silver thread between two high mountains, there in the white sand by the creek you will find the most valuable diamonds.'

"The landowner sold his property as soon as he could, took the money, and spent the rest of his life looking for the diamonds. After an endless and futile search all over the world, he threw himself in a river in disappointment and drowned.

"After the man had moved, the new owner of the property led his camel to a creek for water, when suddenly he caught sight of something gleaming in the white sand. He picked up a large stone with a very special shine; it was as if all the colors of the rainbow poured out of a crack in the stone. He brought the stone to his house and placed it on a shelf for decoration.

"A few days later, the wise man from the East who had visited the previous owner returned. He was invited in the house, saw the stone on the shelf, and exclaimed, 'Why, there is a diamond! Did the old owner return?' The new owner said, 'No, and this cannot be a diamond. It is just a stone I found in my garden.' But the wise man grew serious as he replied, 'I know what a diamond looks like and this is a real diamond.'

"They both ran out to the little creek, which flowed along like a silver thread between two high mountains. They dug in the white sand with their bare hands, and behold! They found one beautiful and precious diamond after the other.

"If only the man had stayed home and looked in his own garden instead of searching elsewhere, he would have found his treasure."

Solomon paused and looked at the Queen of Sheba who put down her wine goblet. He continued, "There are treasures that can only be found in one place in the world. Dig precisely where you stand and you will find valuable treasures and possibilities of all kinds. All of us possess resources that still need to be discovered."

The Queen of Sheba enjoyed the food and Solomon's talent for recounting stories. They folded the blanket, packed what was left of the meal in the basket, and began the ride back to Jerusalem. The wind was refreshing after sitting in the hot sun. A cloud of dust from the road lingered behind them. Suddenly, the queen's horse stopped, spooked by something, and reared. A rattling sound alerted them to a rattlesnake on the road before them.

The Queen of Sheba tried desperately to stay in the saddle as her horse took off in a wild gallop across the field, dodging mulberry trees and big rocks along the way. The sound of the runaway horse's hoofs mixed with the queen's terrified cries. The horse approached a stone wall and instead of jumping over, stopped abruptly. The Queen of Sheba was thrown over the wall, landing on the other side with a dull thud. Everything became quiet.

Solomon followed the queen's horse as fast as he could, but there was nothing he could do to stop the accident. Solomon jumped off his horse before it came to a halt. He leaped over the wall and found the Queen of Sheba lying unconscious and pale on the ground, with blood running from a wound in her forehead. He bent down and prayed aloud, "Dear God, let her live." He put his ear against the queen's chest and heard her heart beating, but she remained unconscious. Solomon jumped to his feet, grabbed the wine goblet from the saddlebag, and rushed back to the queen.

Carefully, he lifted her head and pressed the wine goblet to her lips. A few drops of wine ran down her throat and she coughed. The wine trickled down from the corners of her mouth as she slowly regained the color in her face. She opened her eyes and asked in a low voice, "What happened?"

"Thank God you are alive," said Solomon. "Your horse was spooked by a snake and took off across the field and threw you off. Tell me, can you move your arms and legs?" Despite the pain, the queen was able to move her limbs slightly. "It does not seem anything is broken, but you must stay still. Stay here while I ride for help. It is not far to my palace and I will be back very soon." Solomon placed the picnic blanket under her head and made her as comfortable as possible. Then he quickly mounted his horse and was gone.

A short while later, the sound of many hooves shook the earth as they neared where Solomon had left the queen. Solomon had returned with some of his closest men and one of his most experienced healers. The healer examined the queen, but could not find any injuries except for a small cut on her forehead, which he covered with a bandage. Solomon lifted her carefully in his arms and said, "Even if you seem to have escaped the adventure without injuries, you will ride the rest of the way in my coach." He laid her gently on the seat and the wagon started to move slowly toward home.

In the palace, Solomon assisted the Queen of Sheba to her suite where her attendant became greatly concerned when she heard what had happened. She undressed the queen and gently washed off the dirt. When the Queen of Sheba was resting in her bed, Solomon sat down next to her and said, "Now rest for a while and I will return a little later to see how you are feeling. A guardian angel must have been watching over you." He touched her cheek and then left the room. Exhausted, the queen fell asleep easily.

When the Queen of Sheba opened her eyes, Solomon sat on the edge of her bed watching her. He smiled and inquired how she felt. The queen replied she felt fine except for some stiffness in her arms and legs. She continued, "Just think how strange life is. One moment I enjoyed life and a wonderful ride, and the next moment I was close to death. It is frightening how fragile we are. Life is just an instant of time within two eternities. Tell me, Solomon, are you never afraid to die?"

Solomon thought about this for a moment before he replied, "Naturally, I want to live a long life, but I am not afraid to die. How one lives is more important than how long one lives. I have always tried to live my life as fully as I can, as if each day was the most important day of my life. I have loved and been loved. I have sought wisdom and knowledge, and what I have accomplished feels meaningful to me. I also think I have been of some importance to those closest to me and to my beloved country.

"If a tree falls in the forest and no ear is there to hear it, then is there really a sound? If someone lives and dies without any one paying attention, then did that person really live? The thought of dying may not be as frightening as the feeling that we never really lived, that we reached the end of our lives without really knowing what life was about. But I can also tell you that I am not afraid to die because I know death is the doorway to another existence, a transition to a new life.

"*The path of the godly leads to life. So why fear death?* We all live three lives. The first life lasts nine months in the womb and then we die. Yes, birth is to die from the life we lived for nine months. But it is also the beginning of a new life outside the womb. While we live our second life, our soul lives inside the body, preparing for the third life. Our third life is the eternal life."

> "*The path of the godly leads to life. So why fear death?*"

The Queen of Sheba interrupted Solomon and asked, "But it is difficult to believe in an eternal life. What will it be like?"

Solomon answered, "It is difficult to describe, this is true, because none of us has been there. But imagine that you were able to talk to an unborn child in the womb. You try to describe the world we live in: the clear blue sky, the waves against the shores, the impressive cypress trees, the wonderful fragrant flowers in different colors, and the flight of the powerful eagle. The unborn child might answer, 'It is difficult to believe in the world you describe.'

"But one day the child is born into a world with skies, seas, trees and flowers, people and animals; all the amazing things in our world. In the same way, we will be born into another life after death and discover that it is real.

"When you have overcome your fear of death, you have conquered your biggest enemy, which otherwise would drain you of energy and inner peace. This fear could prevent you from looking forward and doing something meaningful with your life and your possibilities. But when you take your last breath, only your body becomes useless. Your soul lives on. This is the way it is."

Solomon finished speaking and the queen said, "You have almost convinced me. It is my hope that this is what will come to pass someday. But still, something strange has happened. Life seems more valuable when I think of how close I was to death."

Solomon took her hand and said with a soft voice, "It is true. Realizing we only have a short time to live makes life more precious. Death limits our time and creates an awareness that we must live our lives to the fullest."

He stood up and said, "It is best that you rest this afternoon so you can take part in the farewell party tonight."

King Solomon left the room as the sun slowly set, tinting the room with a pink glow. The Queen of Sheba closed her eyes and thought about everything that happened this day. She had come through the terrible accident without serious injuries! She thought about her conversations with Solomon and decided:

———————

"From now on I will go beyond guilt, fear, and worry by daily seeking inner peace. My goal is to create both inward and outward harmony. To achieve peace of mind and harmony I need to overcome my feelings of guilt, fear, and worry. Every day I will forgive everyone I feel has hurt me. I will ask of forgiveness when I have hurt or disappointed anyone, and I will also forgive myself and move on.

"From now on I will love and accept myself just as I am. I am a unique person with a special purpose to give others the gifts I myself need: kindness, love, respect, and the encouragement to grow to my fullest potential.

"From now on I will look at experiences of fear and worry in a more mature and balanced way. I know that facing my fear and worry with courage will help them disappear. I will shift my perspective on death to be more of a reminder to value life and live it fully. This will empower me to seek opportunities in my daily encounters and put my heart and soul into achieving my purpose in life."

———————

My Own Reflections

"I, Wisdom, will make the hours of your day more profitable and the years of your life more fruitful!"

—King Solomon

8

Your Most
Precious Gift

The Queen of Sheba and her attendants walked through the dark garden on their way to Lebanon Forest Hall. As honorable guests of King Solomon, they were to arrive shortly after the other guests had arrived. The herald stood ready to announce their entrance. He opened the door and called out, "The Queen of Sheba and attendants!" as they entered the expansive hall. People gathered in groups, full of expectations, talking, drinking wine, and mingling between the huge alabaster pillars. The murmur of the guests rose toward the ceiling.

Hundreds of oil lamps in golden holders illuminated the dark walls. The windows and wide doors were open toward the garden. A light breeze swept through the assembly hall, carrying with it a fragrance of perfume, incense, and myrrh. The tables were set and an abundance of flowers completed the decor. Bright red pomegranate, fragrant white sycamore from the sycamore fig trees, and a sea of red and yellow lotus flowers adorned the sofas and pillows.

A servant approached the queen, bowed, and respectfully asked her to follow him. They walked through the crowd to the platform, which had been constructed in the back of the hall toward the garden.

They were shown to their seats next to Solomon who was expected to arrive at any minute. All prominent people from King Solomon's government were present. There were Asarja, the high priest, and next to him Josafat who was responsible for the royal archives. The supreme commander of the army, Benaja, who stood a head above all others, was engaged in conversation with Ben-Huhr, the man responsible for the area around Ephraim's mountain district.

Suddenly the clamor softened to a welcome din and the double doors opened. The herald raised his voice, "King Solomon, King of Israel." Solomon crossed the hall accompanied by his royal escorts while the guests bowed in honor. He stopped by the Queen of Sheba and took her hand. Turning to the other guests, he announced, "This farewell party is being held in the honor of the Queen of Sheba. Let us make this a happy and memorable occasion." Then he sat down with the queen to his right in the seat of honor and the talking and laughing joyfully crescendoed.

Still concerned about the queen's fall earlier in the day, he was relieved to hear she was fully recovered, with only a few sore spots.

After a brief moment the feast began. One course after another was served, and the guests feasted, talked, and laughed. Solomon's daughter, Princess Tafat, was seated to the left of the queen. She eagerly pointed out certain guests and excitedly whispered little scandals in the queen's ear.

Once, between courses, Solomon leaned over to Queen of Sheba and began to say something. "Time rushes by …" he said. Then he stopped and said, "Later … later."

After finishing the festive feast, Solomon turned to the Queen of Sheba and suggested, "Let us go for a walk in the garden while the servants clear the tables and prepare for the entertainment. I think we need some fresh air." They left the table and walked through the doors that led to the garden, while the guests glanced at each other knowingly. In the garden, a warm, refreshing breeze frolicked across their skin. It was a beautiful evening and the moon provided soft lighting between the trees. They walked along the stone-covered path by the pond where the insects buzzed above the surface, then were gulped down by the little fish.

"Time passed so quickly since you arrived here," said Solomon. "I want to thank you for everything—for the gifts you brought, and most of all for your company and eagerness to learn. You have really listened to the words of wisdom I wanted to pass on.

"If you did not have your own responsibilities and your own country to rule, nothing could have stopped me from asking you to marry me. Alas, this is not possible, and I can only wish you happiness and blessings in your own life.

You are a good example for all who want to succeed. There are not many female rulers, at least not in the countries I am aware of. You are open and perceptive and have not let yourself be hampered by prejudice or old-fashioned thinking. You came all the way here simply to learn and form connections. I am certain your country will flourish under your leadership. *Without wise leadership, a nation is in trouble; but with good counselors there is safety.*

> *"Without wise leadership, a nation is in trouble; but with good counselors there is safety."*

The Queen of Sheba thanked Solomon for his kind words and expressed her gratitude to have gotten to know him and for all the wisdom he had shared. "I will return to my country with inspiration and happiness in my heart. I now understand that it is possible to have true success in life if one follows the guiding principles you have given me. But I would like to hear what you were going to tell me during dinner. You began with something about time rushing by and I would very much like to hear the continuation."

Solomon turned to the queen and answered, "What I wanted to tell you was this:

"If we want true success in life, we need to use our most precious gift."

"What gift are you thinking of?" asked the Queen of Sheba.

"Our most precious gift is the gift of time," answered King Solomon. He continued, "Time is like a precious jewel you wear. But it has to be protected carefully and worn discreetly, or you will eventually discover it has been stolen. When seconds, minutes, hours, days, weeks, months, and years pass by, they are gone forever. Time can never be called back or made up. A lost day cannot be recovered or replaced by another. Time is our most precious asset, and it is also the most fair. No one can inherit a fortune of time. A king does not own more time than does a slave. A wise man has no more time than a fool. The wealthiest man on earth would not be able to buy more time than anybody else. A day contains the same amount of time for both the rich and the poor. If we spend our time wisely and with great respect, our lives will be filled with opportunities. Each day is hard earned, as we pay for it with a day of our lives.

If you wait for perfect conditions, you will never get anything done. We can only live one day at a time. The fool says, 'I will do it when I have more time.' We will never have more time. We have, and have always had, all the time available. Wasting our time is wasting our lives. The most

> *"If you wait for perfect conditions, you will never get anything done."*

favorable moment to do something will never come; so begin with taking the first step toward your goals today. We build our future one step at a time, day by day.

"*Hard work means prosperity, only a fool idles away his time*. Results and lasting values are created by hard work. If we use our time in the best possible way, we can reach almost any goal. We may have wasted yesterday! We may have wasted today! But we have not yet wasted tomorrow; it is waiting for us like a blank page.

"*It is far better not to say you'll do something than to say you will and then not do it*. Our dreams are meaningless and our words and plans are worthless unless they are followed by action. It is better to begin with a small step than not to begin at all. The right time to act is now! Live your life now. Actions, not words, make dreams come true. It is our own responsibility to create the lives we want to live and to take care of it now! *The wise man will find a time and a way to do what he says. Yes, there is a time and a way for everything.*

"*Better one handful with tranquility than two handfuls with toil and chasing after wind*. To consider time as a valuable resource does not mean that we should hurry and do as many things as we can in one day. It means that we

> "*It is far better not to say you'll do something than to say you will and then not do it.*"

should think more about how to spend our time doing what is really important to us in the longer perspective. To achieve great things, we must always be concentrating on the small number of activities that contribute the greatest value to our lives and our work. We need to set aside time for reflecting and planning and learn to say no to things that waste our time—things that are not important to us. To plan is to let the future into the present so we can start to do something about it today.

"A dull ax requires great strength; be wise and sharpen the blade. We need time to savor our journey. Time to enjoy and remember that we need rest to achieve perspective and gain energy. This is why we should reserve at least one day of the seven days in a week for leisure and inner growth, and listening to our inner being. We need to plan our time so we can work during work hours

> *"A dull ax requires great strength; be wise and sharpen the blade."*

and relax during the time set aside for these purposes. By devoting enough time to think, reflect, and meditate, we can use our time in the best way possible. It will bring progress and balance into our lives.

"I, Wisdom, will make the hours of your day more profitable and the years of your life more fruitful! Life is to be lived to the fullest. When we let our wisdom lead us, we get more value out of each day. We can live a life

that is meaningful and significant, and that means that the world is a little bit different, positively impacted, because we have lived."

Solomon's words became still for a short time and then he continued, "The evening is not over yet. Let us return to the party and enjoy the entertainment and the warm evening."

The sun had set and the stars twinkled above in the black sky. They walked through the leafy garden, where the newly lit lanterns hung from tree branches, lighting the garden path. The fragrances of the garden filled their senses with pleasure. They again passed the fish pond and the guards watching the entrance to the hall. Back in their seats by the table, someone clapped their hands and the entertainment began.

Dancers in thin veils and floor-length hair arrived, playing gold cymbals and tambourines as they moved their hips in an exciting dance. Acrobats and jugglers followed, entertaining the audience with dizzying jumps and tricks to joyous acclamations. There were performances by musicians who sang and played the lyres and harps, and all around them the festivities continued.

When the party was over, the Queen of Sheba thanked King Solomon for the wonderful and memorable evening. "We will begin our journey early in the morning, so it is time to say good-bye," she said with a hint of sadness.

King Solomon answered, "Everything comes to an end sooner or later. Now, return home in peace and share your experiences with your people. I want to give you something, but you must not open it until you are on your way home tomorrow morning." And he handed her a papyrus covered with silk ribbons. "Let the words written here be a reminder of our rewarding conversations."

They said good night and the Queen of Sheba walked through the quiet corridors, lit only by the torchlight by her bedroom. She felt tired and a little dizzy after the farewell party. Before she went to bed she thought about the events of the day and remembered King Solomon's words. She sat down and wrote:

———————

"From now on I will use my most precious gift in the best possible way. I will spend my time with great care so I always do the most important things first. I want to set aside time to maintain balance in my life by renewing my spirit, my body, my soul, and my relationships. By saying YES to what is important in my life and NO to what is unimportant I will move toward my goals in life. It is the small, daily decisions that carry me closer or further from my goals.

"From now on I will try to live one day at a time. Yesterday will never return. I have no guarantee that tomorrow will come. Today is all I have. Time is my most precious gift. Time can never be called back when it is gone. Time can never be saved for later. This moment is the only time that exists.

"From now on I will act, because only action makes dreams come true. What I do now is specific to what

I will become in the very next moment. Each day is a fresh beginning, a new adventure to explore and experience. Just like a sculptor shapes the clay or a painter creates a picture with each draw of his brush, I create my own masterpiece with each action I take. My masterpiece is my life, and I will act NOW!"

My Own Reflections

Epilogue

The hot, vast desert with sand dunes like waves on the sea lay before the caravan. The sun had risen and its warm rays beat down relentlessly. The line of travelers rode through a small village with houses built from dried clay and flat roofs of burnt tiles. This remote village was the starting point for the travelers crossing the desert to southern Arabia. Here, time seemed to have stood still for hundreds of years. One caravan of camels after another arrived or departed from the village. Hectic commerce took place around the warehouses and bazaars, as this was the travelers' last opportunity to purchase necessities before they began the journey across the desert.

The Queen of Sheba and her escorts had left Jerusalem at dawn. Solomon's palace was still covered in darkness and only the light from the stars revealed the contours of the buildings. The camels were loaded with gifts and provisions for the long journey back to Sheba. She thought about the time spent with Solomon and acknowledged feelings of both sadness and gratefulness. It had been a wonderful time.

She found the thick papyrus Solomon gave her the previous night, which she had promised not to read until she was on her way home. She broke the seal, unfolded the sheet, and read:

My dear,

When you read this you will already be en route to your homeland. I am probably sitting in the throne hall, working as usual. I miss you and the void you left feels overwhelming. But it was never meant to be anything more between us than a briefly shared period of time. And our time together was certainly extraordinary.

I remember the day you arrived in my palace as if it happened just this moment: your poise and dignified manner when we were introduced, how we sat on the divan by the throne, and you asked about the right principles for living a successful life. I hold dear all of our conversations, the boat ride, and even the ill-fated horseback ride. I also think of your openness and eagerness to learn. But I believe I am the one who learned the most from you and your demeanor.

You now have with you on your journey home the principles that will create a successful and significant life. I want to remind you of the importance of reflecting over these timeless truths and applying them in your daily life and leadership. It is only when we have made a final decision to take control over our destiny that our self-esteem grows and everything becomes possible. It will be the beginning of a chain of events in the direction of our purpose in life, to serve and contribute to greater value wherever we are.

Do you remember our conversation about how true success originates from inside, how a person may be rich but poor, and poor but rich? To be rich in deeper values that give meaning, contentment, and happiness. We talked about the power of thought, how our thoughts shapes our lives; and to create a vision of our future and pursue it with passion and discipline; how temporary obstacles and adversities are part of life's lessons for us to learn and grow, bringing forth the best in us; that we can only be successful with the support of others, nurturing good relationships understanding that life always gives to the giver. We also talked about the precious gift of time, using it in the best possible way. And the most important of all: to live in harmony with universal principles and let them guide us toward a life with purpose, prosperity, and peace of mind.

I ask you to do the following: each morning when you are meeting the new day, spend some time reading and reflecting over these principles and proverbs. *Take to heart all of them. Every day and all night long they will lead you and save you from harm; when you wake up in the morning, let them guide you into the new day.*

It is now up to you to see the importance of sharing these principles with others, giving them the same opportunity to live truly successful and fulfilling lives. This way you will contribute to their development and growth and you will build bridges of friendship, love, and hope.

You will live forever in my heart!

Solomon

A time for everything:

For everything there is a season,
    a time for every activity under heaven.

A time to be born and a time to die.
    A time to plant and a time to harvest.

A time to kill and a time to heal.
    A time to tear down and a time to build up.

A time to cry and a time to laugh.
    A time to grieve and a time to dance.

A time to scatter stones and a time to gather stones.
    A time to embrace and a time to turn away.

A time to search and a time to quit searching.
    A time to keep and a time to throw away.

A time to tear and a time to mend.
    A time to be quiet and a time to speak.

A time to love and a time to hate.
    A time for war and a time for peace.

Ecclesiastes 3:1–8

TURNING READING INTO ACTION

I recommend that you read the reflection you have made after each chapter, one chapter a day, and deepen your reflection by turning it into actions.

I have prepared a workbook and other material to help you learn more and apply *The Wisdom of Leadership* to your own daily life. You are welcome to look at these materials at my Web site and contact me.

www.perwinblad.com

ACKNOWLEDGMENTS

If I should mention all the people that in some way contributed to this book it would take many pages. My inspiration to write this book has sprung from many sources during my life.

I would like to share my deepest and heartfelt gratitude:

To my lovely family, Pernilla, John, Joanna, and especially my wife Gunilla who always supported me during our many years together. She is the one who has had to bear with my late nights of writing and later reading every word of the manuscript and providing insight and constructive feedback.

To Leif Klingborg, my friend and "coach," whose unselfish support is never ending. His encouragement has lifted me to a higher level.

To Stanley Sjoberg, my pastor in the Centrum Church who inspired me to write during difficult times when my business was hurting back in the recession of 1992.

To all other role models who have inspired my life. Among them is Denis Waitley, whose audiotapes "Psychology of Winning" I listened to almost every day during the early eighties, and Robert H Schuller who I first listened to in Sweden in 1979 at a conference about "Possibility Thinking." I have been to the Crystal Cathedral many times since then listening to his inspiring messages. John C Maxwell and Steven R Covey through their books and teachings are also among leaders and authors I have been inspired by.

ABOUT THE AUTHOR

Per Winblad has built his successful international consulting, coaching, seminar design, and speaking career by practicing the solid leadership principles he presents. The founder of Motivation Consultant Inc., a well respected training firm used by such companies as Ericson and Nokia as well as non-profit organizations to build strong leaders and to help employees perform at their best. To date he has assisted over 5000 managers to greater effectiveness and leadership excellence.

When he speaks, Per both inspires and motivates his audiences while revealing to them the universal guiding principles that contribute to long-term success. He is one of the rare people who has been successful at translating this energy and inspiration to his writing. Per travels extensively presenting leadership principles to audiences and companies worldwide. He lives with his wife in Stockholm, Sweden and has three children and five grandchildren.